IT'S NO
SECRET

IT'S NO SECRET

"The Christian's Guide to God's Law of Attraction"

JAMES PATRICK WATSON DD, CC

Library of Congress Control Number:		2013913961
ISBN:	Hardcover	978-1-4836-7977-8
	Softcover	978-1-4836-7976-1
	Ebook	978-1-4836-7978-5

This book was printed in the United States of America.

Rev. date: 09/26/2013

To order additional copies of this book, contact:
Xlibris LLC
1-888-795-4274
www.Xlibris.com
Orders@Xlibris.com
132125

This book is dedicated to God, God the Father, Son, and Holy Spirit.

It is my sincere hope, prayer, and intention that this book will help you to know each of them better!!

May you have a better relationship with God and by doing so, truly experience God's Law of Attraction firsthand.

James Patrick Watson

CONTENTS

Knowledge is fundamental to attaining real success. Watson sweeps away the clouds of mystery that are associated with "The Law of Attraction". He proves This universal law, as old as time itself, is grounded in scripture, and herein the mystery is removed, giving the reader the tools needed to allow "God's Law of Attraction" to work in our lives. A very informative, useful and interesting read!

Dan Hawkins,
Johnson City, Texas

All who read this book "It's No Secret"—"God's Law of Attraction" are about to receive great personal encouragement for their lives, the lives of their families and all with whom they come in contact! In this book, James Watson, re enforces what our spirits and souls already know and experience but what we often fail to recognize, as a gift from our Creator God. We all too often think of it as our better than average education, or our genes, or even our ego that says we are worthy of these blessings. James gives us clear and concise evidence that God's Law of Attraction is a critical part of God's plan for blessing us with both, all that we can believe for good and for prosperity but also, for all that our Heavenly Father knows that we need, in discipline and correction in our ways.

Those who read "It's No Secret" will relate with the many examples and references, both from scientific sources and from God's Word, that they have personally experienced but was unclear as to why and for what purpose.

It takes courage and a desire for the truth to read such a book. Yet, are we not all seeking a better life, a more abundant life? "It's No Secret" allows the reader to make these discoveries for themselves and does not "push" any one answer upon it's readers.

Yes, the forces of God's Law of Natural Attraction have been working in your life through your parents from before your birth until this moment and beyond, for all of your days. Your reading of James Watson's "It's No Secret" is waiting to bless you and to give you great confidence, in who you are, from where you have come and to where you are going. Comment by: Zester H Hatfield of Timberon New Mexico author of "Job Security In a High-Tech World," "Knights In Shining Armor," "Daddy's Little Girl and Mommy's Little Boy" and "Progressivism Our Road to Serfdom."

Unconditional Support by Zester H Hatfield

It does not take a Sherlock Holmes to see that Dr. Watson, James Patrick, is a passionate advocate of the Law of Attraction. As he has discovered, there are faith-based Christians who believe this Universal Law is New Age. Being a faithful and learned student of his Bible-based faith, James Patrick Watson has created this book to serve as a guide for others to follow along in their Bibles and see the verses and parables within both the Old and New Testaments which demonstrate to all how the Law of Attraction was indeed created by God and applies to all our energies, thoughts and expressions, both positive and otherwise. Dr. Watson practices what he preaches and reaches out to all with his positive message.

James A. McKinnis
San Antonio, Texas

"It's about time". This was my first thought as I began reading Patrick Watson's work on this subject of the law of attraction. For a number of years, especially since the 1930's, Secular humanism has marched steadily to the forefront as an alternative to the moral compass and stable datum upon which this nation was built. That stable datum is enumerated on our coinage as, "In God We Trust" God and his word was, for a great while, the compass which guided our paths. It was the "lamp unto our feet". At first, humanism was simply an additional concept to be considered and given some place alongside these original guiding principles. It wasn't long however until Christians, soundly sleeping while the thief was at work, came to the current state we find ourselves, which is that we now call evil good and good evil. Man has become his own god and man's mind is his law.

Mr. Watson in his work, has systematically undermined, and exposed the humanistic philosophy of this recent interpretation of the law of attraction, and revels to the reader exactly what the law really is, who it's author is, and what it will do for those who have a right standing before God and apply it correctly. It is something of a masterpiece of exposition in laying out the entire argument.

Steve Anderson
Marble falls TX

After reading "It's No Secret," I am reminded of the many blessings we believers take for granted.

Patrick is able to explain God's law of attraction in a way that anyone can follow. You will be blessed with the knowledge that God wants the best for you always and that you just need to receive and share those blessings. This is one book I will reference in the future to be sure. Always seek out what God has in store for you.

Mark Myers
Hallettsville, Texas

IT'S NO SECRET, The Christian's Guide to God's Law of Attraction is a must read for all who desire peace, happiness, health and prosperity. Mr. Watson equips the reader with an understanding of God's Law of Attraction to achieve these goals. He reveals the difference between the humanistic view versus the Christian view, which credits God with its creation, while explaining the science that governs this law in both views. This book answers the age old question posed by skeptics and nonbelievers about why bad things happen to good people and why we see so much suffering in the world. Christians must be armed to answer tough questions such as these. God wants us to be a testimony for His glory and this guide shows us how.

Stacy Dawn Johnson,
Houston Texas author of
"O Brother, Who Art Thou?"

It's No Secret is indeed well thought out with scripture to back up the intent of God's Law of Attraction, with important points revisited many times. A very helpful aid in a time of peril and hardships. I will read it over and over.

Cody Greathouse,
Hye Texas

ACKNOWLEDGMENTS

It is my wish that this book bring God glory and honor as the Creator of the Law of Attraction while providing you an understanding of his law so you may lead positive, productive lives in harmony with God's will and your faith. I feel that although the previous writers have done an outstanding job on the Law of Attraction itself, many Christians view their works as humanistic and contrary to the teachings of the Bible. I believe otherwise, and as a Christian knowing the price that Jesus paid for me, it is my duty to give him his due in this work. Therefore, I have written this guide to demonstrate that the Law of Attraction, rather than being secular or humanistic, is a natural law of God's and is found within the Bible.

In order to demonstrate this, I have used many scriptural references in this book and encourage you to follow along in your Bible and reach your own decision.

As one of the lessons herein is to express gratitude for our blessings, I wish to express thanks first to God the Father for all he provides us each and every moment of our lives. On a personal note, I wish to thank him for allowing me to have been brought up in a Christian home by wonderful parents who gave me Christian love and faith. I also wish to thank my wife, Margie, who is my soul mate and daily shares my life and blessings, also for trusting and believing in me, and encouraging me in pursuing my goals, and above all for being a Proverbs 31 wife. I also want to thank my son Paul for standing firm in his Christian faith and convictions. Because of his rejection to the humanistic views expressed in *The Secret*, I realized there was a need to reveal the Law of Attraction was indeed God's law. I want to thank Jim McKinnis who became a good friend and helped make this book a reality.

I truly hope and pray that you find the answers you are searching for.

May God bless you.
James Patrick Watson, DD, CC

INTRODUCTION

On a national television program about the book *The Secret*, which presented a persuasive albeit humanistic case for the Law of Attraction, when the audience was given a chance to participate, a Christian woman in the audience asked what God's role was within that law.

Regrettably, in my opinion, that question remains unanswered. Christians have not been satisfactorily provided an answer—until now. As a devout Christian and student of the scriptures, accepting God's truth, I have researched the Bible extensively and have come to conclude the Law of Attraction is indeed God's law. Therefore, I would like this guide to resolve the conflict those Christians have when they fear that accepting and using the Law of Attraction is contrary to following their faith in God and in the Bible.

I first heard of the Law of Attraction by that name from the publicity surrounding a 2006 book, *The Secret*, written by Rhonda Byrne, based on an earlier film of the same name. The more I studied her book and read others dealing with the Law of Attraction, although in some cases referring to in different ways and written prior and since, and reflected on what I learned, I determined the "secret" as she called it was no secret at all but was very much in line with my faith, the faith I discovered from my earliest readings of the Bible and have followed since. Yet when I attempted to share this discovery with many of my Christian friends and family, I found that their most common response was to reject "the secret" as secular, humanistic, New Age, therefore something that Christians should not be watching or reading. While I understood how they came to this conclusion about the author's "Law of Attraction," for she did not give God and the Bible their due, I also became concerned they were doing themselves harm in their misunderstanding. I felt it was not the Law of Attraction that was wrong but that they're not "seeing" it within the Bible. Believing as I did, God gave me the confidence that I could and should reveal to others; with the Bible as my support, I began to think of writing this book as a guide to helping others.

The more I continued to research many other books and articles about the Law of Attraction, both positive and critical, I became even more convinced the Law of Attraction is as demonstrable a law of God's as is the Law of Gravity. I came to believe it was God's mission for me to write this *guide* to share my discovery with many others. I wanted this guide to be not only for those whose faith was firmly founded in the Bible but also for those who were still searching to understand how fundamental and all-encompassing God's love and power is and always will be so that they might find their own faith. I wish to reveal to you, the reader, my conclusions and point out within the Bible how I came to those conclusions. I believe this can provide you a blueprint for accepting the Law of Attraction as indeed a law of God's and encourage you to build your own foundation so that you may receive the blessings God has in store for you.

In this guide, I will begin by answering this question first: what is the Law of Attraction? Simply stated, the Law of Attraction is God's power everywhere in the universe that draws similar energies together. As the light of the sun provides life to plants, positive energies attract positive outcomes, as is the will of God. We understand and accept gravity as a natural law that affects all our lives whether we believe in it or not. So by understanding how God's Law of Attraction works, you can begin to understand how it positively affects your lives. However, as positive energies attract positive energies, the opposite is also true; negative thoughts and energies also attract negative energies and outcomes. So by misunderstanding and rejecting this natural law of God's, you may in effect attract the opposite of the abundance God intends for you. I believe that after you see how the Law of Attraction works, you can align yourself with God's energies to draw into your life what God wishes to bless you with.

I again remind you that you can follow in your Bible and be assured that the Law of Attraction is there within the scriptures. I will highlight specific verses in both the Old Testament and the New Testament for you to read along and decide.

I will point out how God's Law of Attraction works so that you can better avoid misinterpretations and understand what you must do to truly receive God's blessings. We understand, for example, what electricity can do for us in our own houses; but we must also take precautions to ensure that the wiring is adequate and circuit breakers are in place so that the electrical energy works for us and not cause a fire or other hazards. I will illustrate how our spiritual being should be centered and in line with God's for us to be truly blessed. How we do this is by following the Bible first and finding therein the guidance to maintain our spiritual center. In following the Bible, we confirm who God the Creator is and who man is as well as how God created the universe. We also understand that God is perfect and that man is imperfect. We can and should *ask* God for his blessings, but we do not *tell* God what to do for us. God will provide us the blessings, but our wishes must be in line with his will. This simply requires faith.

I will show you in the Bible how Jesus himself teaches the Law of Attraction, referring to specific verses for you to see how beautifully he sets it forth for you to follow. I believe that by listening to the voice of the Holy Spirit, you can renew your mind by knowing God and be ready to follow God's plan for you. You will learn to appreciate the beauty of being still and understanding God and the universe. By doing so, not only will you become ready to receive your blessings, but you will also joyfully use those blessings to bring God's blessings to others.

In this guide, I also address certain misunderstandings, questions, and criticisms of others about how God's Law of Attraction works. We must caution ourselves to understand the difference between the ends and the means. I will provide you with many examples you can consider and help overcome your fears and concerns.

You will find throughout, the guide repeatedly makes many points in different chapters. I do this since they should be emphasized and reinforced because of their importance in understanding God's intent for you. I apologize in advance to those who feel I appeared to be repeating the same lessons excessively.

As my wish in the guide is to reveal to you what the Law of Attraction is in the universal sense and how it is indeed God's law and firmly rooted in the biblical verse, I believe it is necessary to also provide you examples of how it is involved in your daily life. I feel that by using examples in my own life, I can personalize it to reveal what I believe it is and how I came to believe as I do.

In 2005, I married my soul mate, my wife, Margie. She has been a major blessing to me, and I thank the Lord daily for our blessings. I have a very clear recollection of a beautiful day during our courtship when we were enjoying a picnic by the nearby Guadalupe River. During that beautiful afternoon, I took a few minutes and told her the dreams and goals that I had at that time.

There were five goals that I listed that day. They were to build our house using an old barn on our property; to create and grow my business Rustic Art Gallery, my custom log furniture business; to get a Dodge 4x4 diesel pickup; to build an airstrip on our ranch and buy an airplane to go along with it; and, lastly, to get a place in New Mexico.

Over the next five years, the only thing that did not happen was buying a plane. However, I did build a grass strip and made a trade with my instructor, and I am now learning how to fly, all preparatory to getting that plane. Everything else came to pass.

Then in 2010, I faced some struggles; and finally, it dawned on me I had not reset the bar. I had not set new goals to replace the ones that had come to pass. That was a very important lesson.

The next two years, I knew God was leading me, but I was not sure where yet. It was a time of personal growth. I sometimes felt like my head was going to burst wide open because of all the stuff I was putting in. It was around this time that this book began forming in my mind. I had already read *The Secret* and other books, each seeming to recommend further reading to answer questions that would pop up. I cannot say how many books I found on the "Free Shelf" at a nearby community library that either were recommended or answered my questions that had come up. I learned that when you are ready for the answer, God will provide it to you. In addition to the library, I perused a local used-book store as well as thrift stores and flea markets to continue my search for answers. As a result, I kept adding books to my collection, but I love to read anyway, and my personal library means a lot to me.

As the book idea grew in my mind, I felt God was still leading me. In April 2012, I received an honorary Doctor of Divinity Degree. I also enjoyed sharing my discoveries with others, and in July of 2012, I became a certified life coach. Although I still was not sure where God was taking me, it started to become a little clearer in the last few months of 2012. In September of 2012, I had a very bad case of vertigo, which kept me from working for over three months. I had a lot of time for reflection, although for the first month, I could not read more than a few minutes. All I could do was think and reflect. I had in the past been complimented on my voice and never had had a problem with public speaking but had never pursued it. Around this time, it started to sink in. I was reminded about the scripture of Jesus talking about talents, a type of coin at that time, and began to realize it is also true of the gifts and natural talents that God gives us are ours to use and celebrate his goodness. That was when some things started to clear up for me.

This book is the result of that reflection. I truly hope and pray that I can use my discoveries about the Law of Attraction to reveal to Christians and others alike that it is no secret, it is in the Bible, and it is indeed God's Law of Attraction.

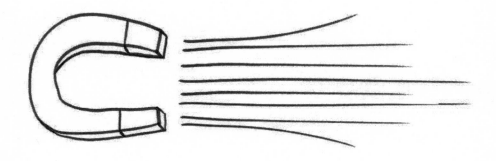

The thief cometh not, but for to steal, and to kill, and to destroy: I am come that they might have life, and that they might have it more abundantly.

John 10 v 10

CHAPTER 1

What Is the Law of Attraction?

"I attract to my life whatever I give my attention, energy and focus to, whether positive or negative."

—*Michael Losier*

Although the Law of Attraction is a natural law, for most people, it became part of the popular culture in 2007 following the publication of Rhonda Byrne's book, *The Secret*, which was followed by a film of the same name. The author appeared twice on the Oprah Winfrey show, and the book went on to become one of the most popular best-sellers in the history of publishing. The title refers to the author's assertion that over the ages, certain people knew of a secret power unknown to the vast majority that enabled them to prosper. The *secret* they had discovered is in fact a natural law of God's universe and enabled them to attract power, wealth, and success into their lives. That law is the Law of Attraction. One can do even elementary research on the Law of Attraction and confirm that there were many others who in one way or another had written of this power (example: http://en.wikipedia.org/wiki/Law_of_attraction). Yet Ms. Byrne's book gained her amazing success; and, in fact, it has become so successful as to generate an industry of its own as others have taken up the movement to not only write their own views and promote the Law of Attraction in numerous ways, workshops, classes, and other coaching and counseling ventures. Her book also has generated considerable comment and criticism, both positive and negative, because some are referring to the scientific claims as "pseudo-science" and others are challenging the notion that we "attract" our own fate through this power, asking rhetorically whether the starving children of Africa, for example, consciously wish to starve. No one will question that anyone who reads this far in this book is thousands of times more blessed than most of the world. To those critics of the Law of Attraction who refer to the less fortunate, I suggest that perhaps God is asking those of us who are far more blessed to use the Law of Attraction to benefit also those who are less fortunate than ourselves. Since seeing her movie and reading her book, I concluded the Law of Attraction is in fact one of God's laws. Also, after much reflection and further research as well as conversations with others, I began to feel it important to point out that following the Law of Attraction should not create a conflict for Christians as it is right there in the Bible as I will show you later in this guide. I wish to give God his due. I also want to address some of the criticisms leveled by the naysayers later as well.

Simply stated, the Law of Attraction is God's power everywhere in the universe that draws similar energies together. These energies can be manifested in the form of prayers, thoughts, ideas, people, situations, and circumstances; but, ultimately, they are energies that attract like energy. Most people have experienced an example of this energy when they see an envelope in the mail, and they have a "sense" of what is inside, either a positive or negative sense, and opened it to find what they sensed was true. Another simple example is the thought of a person and moments later hearing the phone ring, and it is the person whom they had just thought of. We also have medical evidence of people whose positive attitudes have overcome serious illnesses in mysterious ways, which have defied explanations. They have in fact "attracted" the beneficial results others had not thought possible. Often we refer to these circumstances as *miracles;* and sometimes they do appear miraculous for one to overcome others' negative outlooks, opinions, and energies. Whether the person acknowledges their divine origin or not, these miracles do come from God. We have daily evidence of this if we open our eyes, and center and nourish our own spiritual beings. Even the American Cancer Society on its website mentions a variation of this, referring to one of the most popular examples, the "cure" famous *Saturday Review* editor Norman Cousins acknowledged after his recovery from cancer (http://www.cancer.org/ treatment/treatmentsandsideeffects/complementaryandalternativemedicine/ mindbodyandspirit/humor-therapy; http://www.ncahf.org/articles/c-d/cousins. html). While no responsible individual would or should recommend that one rely solely on any of the variations of the overall Law of Attraction, one can suggest the converse as well; and that is that one adopts a negative attitude and abandons hope or belief in powers or cures beyond those we own, prescribe, or otherwise "control" or dispense. I suggest that the person who says or believes he cannot do something will certainly succeed . . . at not doing it! One who on the other hand thinks, "I believe I can do this . . ." will try and will at the very minimum give himself the chance of actually doing it. After all, according to some folklore, a German aerodynamics expert told another scientist that his calculations proved a bumblebee could not physically generate the lift to fly. Fortunately, the bumblebee does not read and cannot be bothered. The author of the following provides both the story and discounts it as folklore, but it still suggests that some experts can be wrong (http://www.straightdope.com/columns/read/1076/is-it-aerodynamically-impossible-for-bumblebees-to-fly).

There is a temptation when one wants to tell his story; he gets so excited that he gets ahead of himself. That's the case here; there are times when I may have to mention something and get back to it later to fully explain it. I hope that when I do that, the explanation will make better sense in context. However, I would like to expand on the point that I wanted to make with the bumblebee story. My purpose is not to mock or discredit scientists or science but to suggest that there is ample evidence over the centuries that we, as man, have not had all the answers and that the experts often had to admit their errors. So the fact that some scientist will dispute another's view of the universe should not be assumed to make the observation wrong. As I wrote, in my view, there is more than enough evidence to support my conclusion that the Law of Attraction is as much a natural law as is the Law of Gravity.

No one in his right mind will ask another person, "Do you believe in the Law of Gravity?" without raising serious questions about his mental well-being. Even the most skeptical person does not ask another person holding a brick above the doubter's bare foot to drop it and say, "Show me (him) gravity . . ." But in truth, we do not really "see" gravity but the effects of energy that attracts the object to fall. We are all cautious enough to understand that there are also other energies that possess amazing and potentially dangerous results if we do not take precautions. We protect, especially our youngest children whose first efforts at crawling around their living rooms to explore their expanding world combined with the curiosity they possess from infancy by putting safeguards on electrical outlets because we know the dangers of electricity. Yet we in truth only see evidence of the energy rather than "electricity" itself. We take these things for granted and do not question these energies and their applications and hazards any more than we would purposefully jump off a cliff to "test" the Law of Gravity.

Our knowledge sometimes is not discovered easily nor does everyone "see" the outcomes at the same time. Until not that long ago, even most of the early scientists would have said, "Birds fly. Man does not." A literal interpretation of that even today might be true in the sense that I cannot flap my arms as a bird does and fly to New York or even up to the neighbor's tree. In fact, I can "fly" to New York and quite a bit faster than a bird, truth be told.

Let's think about the above example a bit more in a different sense. First, there were the dreamers who saw the birds flying and imagined or "visualized" what it would be like to do so. Over the centuries, there were some others with similar dreams and visualizations, who might have also seen how smoke appeared to defy the Law of Gravity by rising into the sky and they began to wonder, "What if . . ." Hot air balloons soon followed, taking intrepid adventurers into the sky, but still most scientists would have been hard-pressed to make the jump from that bag of hot air to the Wright Brothers successfully flying a winged aircraft made of fabric, cables, and sticks, a distance of less than the wingspan of a Boeing 747.

Some of our more recent scientific discoveries are demonstrating to scientists a "disturbing" pattern that "hard science" has sought to deny or disprove, as there is more and more evidence revealing scientific truths and spiritual beliefs in the same discovery. Perhaps none is more evident of this than quantum mechanics, whose early history puzzled researchers and flew in the face of their nineteenth-century laws of physics, suggesting entirely new "rules" (http://en.wikipedia.org/wiki/History_of_quantum_mechanics). Now this bizarre behavior is being confirmed in research, with results that almost defy physical reality. I don't even pretend to be able to comprehend it, but to one who took a course in high school physics a generation ago, it certainly sounds virtually contradictory to all the hard truths and physical laws, theorems, and axioms they always taught as hard and fast "laws." In fact, one could easily suggest that it sounds far more like a spiritual law, certainly than gravity for example. For certain, this means we should keep an open mind to how God's universe works.

I want to suggest that in understanding and accepting the Law of Attraction as a natural law, we should take this wider view of natural laws as laws that we can "see" and accept in the daily world. By opening our eyes and minds much as scientists are admitting they have to, we can better appreciate the connections we might otherwise overlook. We also have to caution ourselves to avoid either the conclusion that we fully understand the law or try to simplify our concepts and mislead ourselves. Even as Christians, we must not forget our relationship to God and the universe. As we know through the Bible, God is perfect. He created the universe and everything within it. He is and always will be. All knowledge discovered and to come is and has always been his to know. Obviously, I will refer to the Bible more and more as I continue, but I wish to insert two verses, the first from Isaiah 2:11: *"The haughty looks of man shall be brought low, and the lofty pride of men shall be humbled, and the LORD alone will be exalted in that day."* Even the wisest man or woman on this planet has imperfect knowledge, and the Bible cautions him to avoid pride and hubris, the arrogance of "knowing everything there is to know" and dismissing other points of view.

The second is from *Mark 12:17: "And Jesus answering said unto them, Render to Caesar the things that are Caesar's, and to God the things that are God's. And they marveled at him."* God has given the creatures of the earth, including man, so much; and through free will, he has allowed man to decide how to conduct his life, whether in accordance with the Bible and the scriptures, or otherwise. In this verse, I suggest that we take the word to remind us that there are man's creations, rules, and beliefs and that we must not confuse the difference between man's and God's realms and acknowledge to God his kingdom and his laws.

In the introduction, I recalled the five goals I expressed to my beloved and how they came to pass. I wish to repeat this to suggest what the Law of Attraction is and what it is not. I expressed to her, and to God and the universe, my goals. But I did not simply sit back and wait for them to happen. Instead, by having set righteous goals and working toward them, I suggest I also "attracted" those goals. I use the examples of the truck I wanted as well as the New Mexico property I had visualized and wanted for us. In addition to the 4x4 Dodge truck, my wife was actually given a 4x4 GMC Yukon. We also then found a property for sale on eBay and obtained a very favorable owner-financed zero-interest transaction that enabled us to acquire a wonderful place where I take my son and grandsons camping. In fact, on the first occasion, on such a camping trip three weeks after we got it, I noticed an alligator juniper tree and looking around saw the place was covered with them. My son and I loaded up the truck and brought back my first of several truckloads since, wood that I have used to make furniture that has paid about two-thirds the cost of the land! I had no idea when we bought the place that it would produce such a bounty of wood without even cutting any live trees.

Then, a year after buying the first place, some very good friends called and asked if we would be interested in another place in western New Mexico, ten and a half acres with a cabin already on the property, which they wanted to trade. So we wound up with two places in New Mexico, places we can flee to escape the Texas summer heat and share with our family and friends.

While I mentioned not yet having my own airplane, I believe that this too will become part of our lives when the time is right. In the meantime, I have worked to clear an airstrip on the ranch and met a pilot who is providing me lessons in trade for keeping his planes at the ranch as well as advising me on the type of aircraft that would best suit our needs.

Earlier, I mentioned how I realized after achieving a number of the goals I had described to my wife, Margie, in 2005. By 2010, I became aware

I needed to reset the bar, to seek new goals. This book therefore is the manifestation of one of my new goals set in 2011.

I believe I can truly state without a doubt that the above personal experience reveals much of what I believe it takes for the Law of Attraction to work for us. But it is important to understand how it might work against us if we do not understand and accept what the Law of Attraction is. Our own energies might be conscious or unconscious and sometimes contradictory. While a person might consciously state and believe they want to lose weight or live a healthier lifestyle, they might sabotage those goals by fearing or actually doing the opposite, either by not understanding the nature of the process or by simply taking actions contrary to those goals. One who, for example, wishes to lose twenty pounds must accept the reality that this would involve a change, exercising, and eating wisely day by day rather than by feverishly attempting to accomplish the goal through shortcuts and, failing, returning to the previous unhealthy practices. Man, though imperfect, can choose whether to attract positive or negative energies and, seeing how God's Law of Attraction works, can choose that path. But there are naysayers whom we all encounter. Ironically, even skeptical scientists whose predispositions were to disprove the mysterious energy or Law of Attraction have actually come to acknowledge the law exists. Each time they believed otherwise, they have been proved wrong, not only about the Law of Attraction but also by many other "laws" of nature and science they claimed. For centuries, they stated the sun was the center of the universe and the atom indivisible only to find themselves wrong. Today they continue to probe the inner and outer reaches of the universe, and although they have attempted to find other answers otherwise, their research to the farthest reaches of space or the most elementary compositions within the atom, they have come to concede that everything is composed of energy and vibrations, the rate of vibration being the essential difference. Even in studying the human mind, they also have discovered that our thoughts demonstrate similar electrical energies, both positive and negative. Not everyone who has explored this law describes it in the same manner, nor do they agree either in terms of the scientific theories or explanations, but most have to admit that indeed it does affect our lives, however mysteriously.

The Law of Attraction has been described in various terms in the past, perhaps the most well known is the power of positive thinking. There are many who have written of this power from various starting points as well, ranging from those who approached the subject in practical terms, such as one of the earliest, Wallace D. Wattles in *The Science of Growing Rich*.

"A great attitude is not the result of success; success is the result of a great attitude."

—*Earl Nightingale*

The Bible speaks of our fruit, both good and bad. There are many biblical verses that attest to this. When we speak or have negative thoughts, we are in fact bringing about "bad fruit" often without realizing the bad fruit has in fact been "attracted" by our own negative energies. Conversely, good thoughts and wishes and maintaining our faith in God through the Bible allows us to harvest good fruit, which we seek; and this in turn strengthens our faith.

In Matthew 9:20-22:

"20And, behold, a woman, which was diseased with an issue of blood twelve years, came behind him, and touched the hem of his garment:

21For she said within herself, If I may but touch his garment, I shall be whole.

22But Jesus turned him about, and when he saw her, he said, Daughter, be of good comfort; thy faith hath made thee whole. And the woman was made whole from that hour."

The woman had heard that Jesus was coming, and she had heard of how he had healed others. She believed that if she could just touch his garment, she would be healed despite the twelve years of "bad fruit" in her blood tissue. She had faith in Jesus and, in her faith, spoke to heal herself and did so. Jesus comforted her, acknowledging that it was her faith that had healed her, and from that moment forward, she was healed and bore good fruit. I would like to point out that this series of verses is the first time a person was healed by touching his garment. After this, many people were healed by touching his clothes.

There are many, many instances within the Bible where Jesus counsels us to have faith. The following three verses in Mark 11, I believe, are wonderful examples.

In Mark 11:

"22And Jesus answering saith unto them, Have faith in God.

*[23]For verily I say unto you, That whosoever shall **say** unto this mountain, Be thou removed, and be thou cast into the sea; and shall not doubt in his heart, but shall **believe** that those things which he **saith** shall come to pass; he shall have whatsoever he **saith**.*

[24]Therefore I say unto you, What things so ever ye desire, when ye pray, believe that ye receive them, and ye shall have them."

When I looked at verse 23, I realized all of a sudden we all have mountains in our lives. So I ask you, the reader, what is your mountain that you wish to throw into the sea? I also wish to point out that in these three verses, Mark repeats the word "say" three times while using the word "believe" only once. After reflecting on this, I feel that he repeated "say" while not "believe" to reveal to us that while we believe and have faith in God, we must also "say" or speak our belief, our faith, to demonstrate our faith positively. We cannot, for example, "believe in the positive" on the one hand but "say" negative thoughts. We must state our faith, the faith we believe, openly and confidently and positively to fully throw the mountains that afflict us into the sea.

God's Law of Attraction, which is right here in the Bible, requires you to indeed have faith; and by having that faith, you can attract the bounty God has in store for you.

"Sometimes faith is knowing that you will make it through. It's believing in abundance and your own worthiness."

—Oprah Winfrey

Again, I also suggest to Ms. Winfrey that we also state our faith in our own worthiness and abundance within the spirit of the Lord.

For those of us whose faith in the Bible has never failed us, we might smile. In all their research to prove otherwise over the centuries, they have come to confirm "scientifically" the omnipresence of God, the Creator of the universe. God created that energy. He is that energy.

God created man in his image just as he created the universe and everything in the natural world. He also created and gave to man the unique gift among his many creatures to discover and understand God's laws and create his own fate by adhering to those laws and benefitting from the fruits of his own labor. It is important to understand this distinction. Animals, for example, know to avoid the dangers of gravity; and many, for survival, are given remarkable skills and capacities to climb sheer cliffs or fly across bodies of water with navigation skills we as humans do not possess. Yet through our unique gift from God, we can use our understanding of the laws and application of learned techniques, defy gravity, and fly across the globe, landing safely where we wished to travel. But in fact we understanding and working within God's laws, fully aware that God's Law of Gravity still applies. We gain when we observe and respect and work within God's laws—laws that God intends to provide well-being and abundance if followed.

Yet he also gave man free will. By doing so, he gave man the choice of understanding or ignoring his laws, of following good or evil. We are given the scriptures, which contain the commandments as well as counsel and examples of God's will for us. He cautions us against false pride and vanity by reminding us of the lilies of the field, whose natural beauty is beyond the ability of worldly kings to achieve. Man is imperfect and, through his expression of free will, is permitted to follow or ignore, to honor and respect God, or to turn away as a nonbeliever.

While I have found their objection true in the sense that most of the many who have written about the Law of Attraction in their own works have taken a humanistic approach that discourages many devout Christians from going further, learning more, and discovering how the Law of Attraction "works" and understanding how not only is it a natural law as much as the Law of Gravity, which Christians naturally accept as God's law within his creation of the universe and everything herein, and whereas the Law of Gravity is physical, the Law of Attraction can be seen to be spiritual and confirmed within the scriptures.

Our positive thoughts or energies draw or attract positive outcomes, actions, and events; and, conversely, our negative thoughts and energies, whether conscious or otherwise, generate negative results. By understanding and accepting this as one of God's laws and putting forth positive energy, prayers, and wishes, we renew our minds, attract Christian wishes, and let the Holy Spirit guide and direct us in everything we do, trusting that the results will be positive. Regrettably, the opposite is also true—negative thoughts and fears also "attract" negative outcomes. Many Christians have judged the Law of Attraction as presented in most popular media to be humanistic and have therefore judged it to be antithetical to their faith. By misunderstanding and rejecting this natural law of God's, we will in effect attract the opposite of the abundance God intends for us.

Above all, we must accept that we are, as humans, imperfect beings while God the Creator is perfect; and as such, ours is not to question God's will.

Let's look at the Law of Gravity. Do we "question" it? Certainly not! We accept it as one of God's natural laws. As such, we know it applies to us, whether Christian or otherwise. Two individuals, one a Christian, the other an agnostic, standing on the edge of a cliff, if they fall, will be equally affected, regardless of their faith, at least in this lifetime. We accept and understand it and act accordingly. Yet we cannot "see" gravity in the strictest sense. Because we see the effects of gravity so easily in our daily lives, we accept its physical presence as a law without seeing or truly understanding the physical energy called gravity. Even scientists cannot define what energy is, although they can measure what it does, how it acts. By doing so, we lead safer, more productive lives. But we cannot choose to accept or ignore gravity except at our own peril.

To truly understand and accept the Law of Attraction is more challenging because it is far more spiritual, and although it often manifests itself physically as in abundance, it cannot be seen so easily as the effects of gravity. Most of us have experienced situations in which a person, perhaps a stranger, although acting friendly or gently, gives us a sense of discomfort. We "know" it is best to avoid that person, although we cannot provide physical "evidence" of how we came to our decision. Many of us have seen a pet dog growl at a person, although he or she is smiling, seemingly harmless. I think that our pets and even we are in fact sensing a negative energy on their part that, although less easy to describe, is as real as other natural energies.

We ourselves may be guilty of being the source of negative energy without realizing it. Doubt and fear are largely negative emotions or energies. Often, although we consciously want a good result and hope that it will occur, we fear that it will not and are disappointed when it does not happen. None of us are foolish enough to believe that by simply "wishing" to win a lottery will mean that we expect to do so, and we also are sensible enough to understand that although we might "see" the house of our dreams in our mind, we need a lot of planning and work and good fortune to actually have that roof over our heads in our future.

None of us are foolish enough to feel we can command God to suspend the Law of Gravity so we can fly without wings or jump off the roof of a building without incurring great harm to ourselves. By the same light, failing to understand and accept the Law of Attraction can result in our failing to receive the blessings God has in store for us. Let me show you more about how God's Law of Attraction works.

NOTES

NOTES

LOVE

FRIENDS

COMFORT

HEALTH

FAMILY

HAPPINESS

For as he thinketh in his heart, so is he: Eat and drink, saith he to thee; but his heart is not with thee.

Proverbs 23 v 7

CHAPTER 2

How Does the Law of Attraction Work?

"What you radiate outward in your thought, feelings, mental pictures, and words, you attract into your life."
—*Catherine Ponder*

It is very important to understand how the Law of Attraction works and how it *does **not*** work. First let's consider the words of a number of other writers who have taken this on.

The Law of Attraction is described by numerous voices on the subject as working like a magnet, attracting similar energies, vibrations, frequencies as a magnet draws iron particles to itself. Gravity could be described in much the same way in that it attracts objects to the center of the body, exerting the force, the energy called gravity. Of course, in principle, all physical bodies in the universe exert gravity; but it obviously is only seen in a measurable manner in large bodies, such as the earth, the moon, and the sun, rather than people and buildings, which physically are far too insignificant to demonstrate a measurable force. We are told, for example, that the moon's gravity on its surface is approximately one-sixth of the force of gravity on this earth. A larger planet, say Jupiter, would exert far greater force than we experience here on earth. Deepak Chopra, seeking to compare the two writes, "People use it (the Law of Attraction) like a wish magnet. They bait the hook with a dream, toss it out into the universe, and expect to draw in money, a soul mate, happiness, whatever big fish they want to land. But think about another natural law: gravity. Gravity isn't selective. It pulls on everything, not just the things you want it to pull (http://www.oprah.com/spirit/How-the-Law-of-Attraction-Works-Ask-Deepak).

He is pointing out that we need to understand that the Law of Attraction, just like the Law of Gravity, is always with us; and we must understand it requires more than simply "using it" when we think it is convenient. When we are working on the roof of a house, for example, we caution ourselves to be careful not to slip because we could easily tumble off the roof and injure ourselves or worse. We cannot simply "wish" gravity away to suit us.

I am reminded of the story of two farmers whose plots of land are side by side and similar in size. One of the farmers gets up early, works hard all day, and does all the things necessary so that his land and animals reward him and his family with abundance. The second gets up a little later and does not quite work the land with the same devotion; and, as a result, his harvests are less, and his life is not quite so prosperous. Often, taking a break for lunch, they will stand on either side of the fence that separates their farms and discuss their lives. They were both God-fearing family men, and their talks usually revolved around the world they knew. On many occasions, the harder-working farmer would describe how his cow might have borne him twin calves and still produced enough milk, butter, and cheese for his family, or how his crop had been especially good that year, not bragging, just mentioning it. Every time, his friend would comment, "God has really blessed you" or something similar, reflecting that the farmer's abundance was a blessing from the Almighty. The prosperous farmer would nod and acknowledge God's blessings and express his gratitude. This went on time after time until one day the prosperous farmer, hearing his friend's usual comment about God's blessing him, paused and said, "You know, we got our farms just about the same time, didn't we?" The first farmer reflected a moment and nodded. "You remember how my farm didn't look so good back then, weeds and brush everywhere." Again, the farmer nodded. "Well, God wasn't doing such a great job by himself back then, was he?"

It took the other farmer a moment to get the point. Yes, God provided us the bountiful land, but we also had to do our part, clearing the land, working hard. I liked how this story brought home the oft heard saying, "God helps those who help themselves."

Another writer makes a very important contribution when he writes the following, "the Law of Attraction works on the principle of energy vibrations" and defines this energy as "thoughts married to emotions emit (these) vibration(s)" (http://www.squidoo.com/TheLOAWorks#module55012662).

His point is in my opinion very important; it is not just our conscious thoughts or wishes but also our unconscious ones that he labels "emotions," which combine to create the energy and emit the vibrations. He continues,

"I'm sure you've been around people with bad vibrations standing in line at the grocery store or wherever. Don't you find yourself moving away from them? Though you may not know it, you are emitting energy vibrations right back to the universe, which . . . (sends) you the same thing that you're putting out."

Deepak Chopra, in the same article I mentioned earlier, points to some reasons why our emotions might be sending these unintended vibrations, citing stress, anxiety, and depression as three causes that could result in our not attract what we thought we had consciously sought. "The Law of Attraction . . . pulls on everything; it attracts to you many things at once, not just one thing."

A third writer states, "Before we understand how to use the Law of Attraction, it's important to notice how the Law of Attraction is already working in your present life. It's only when you notice how the Law of Attraction works that you will be able to understand how to start using it 'deliberately' for your benefit" (http://www.outofstress.com/law-of-attraction-work/).

This last point I feel is critical to my message and wishes for you. Whether you consciously accept the Law of Attraction and how it works, it is **already** working in your life. So by understanding how you are "attracting" the life you are presently living, you also become empowered to improve your life dramatically.

As you may notice in the above writers' descriptions of how the Law of Attraction works, they do **not** credit God or the Bible specifically. There are many writers who do mention the Bible and other spiritual writings of the past perhaps, but many Christians interpret that those writers are not giving God his due, and the lack of directly acknowledging God and the Bible indicates that the Law of Attraction is therefore antithetical to their faith. I truly believe God has given me the mission of proving otherwise, and the writing of this guide is the means to do this.

We as Christians know that God is perfect, and man is imperfect. None of us would dispute this. So acknowledging our imperfection, we also must acknowledge that we should refrain from judging others or from being too vain and proud and assuming we know better what God intends for us.

Again, I will repeat myself. The Law of Attraction, although a spiritual law far more than a physical one, still works much as the Law of Gravity. If we step off a cliff, willingly or otherwise, we will fall and very likely cause ourselves great harm or worse, regardless of whether we are Christians, Muslims, or atheists. But what about when we "see" that the Law of Gravity isn't all that infallible? I'll use this amusing example from a while back. There was often a lot of laughter in class when a science teacher would tell the young students how gravity would attract a feather just as much as a hammer. The young students laughed because they thought they could "see" that was not true; the feather would float down, while the hammer would hit the flour loudly. Of course, here on our earth, we have some conditions that seem to appear to modify our understanding because we can "see" for ourselves. The astronaut David Scott of Apollo 15 finally put the matter to rest when he was on the moon's surface by dropping a feather and hammer on camera, and they hit the surface at the same time (http://www.youtube.com/watch?v=KDp1tiUsZw8). It is fun to watch even almost forty years later.

I suggest that the lesson we should take from the amusing Apollo video is that sometimes we "see" or misinterpret something and think that this shows the "law" does not work. Sometimes we are the ones misinformed.

One thing I hope to make perfectly clear is that I in no way want to suggest to you that I have always made the right decisions, never been at fault, or never made mistakes. Hopefully, I continue to learn and pray and follow God's words in the Bible.

I want to get closer to home and suggest to you that whether you have understood the Law of Attraction and how it works, there have been examples in your own lives that I suggest you have experienced, which demonstrate this law.

For example, there are people I have known who, regardless of what has happened in their lives, hardships they have faced, have maintained a positive outlook and expressed gratitude to God. They rarely complain and almost never dwell on whatever hardships they face. These people don't necessarily have more money or better jobs than others, yet they smile rather than frown. For my part, I like being around these people because their "energy and vibrations" indeed make me feel better. They seem to want to get up and tackle another day and do better than the day before.

Conversely, there are other people I have known who start the day with a complaint, a negative attitude, expressing the "fact" that something bad is going to happen to them. Some of these people I have known have nice houses, make decent money, and yet are unhappy. Even if they get that proverbial check in the mail, they'll find fault, it should have been more, I'll just have to spend it on bills, whatever. Even if they give lip service to God, go to church on Sundays, and want to have better lives, they seem to neither be happy or grateful. Truthfully, I find it challenging to be around these people because their negative energy is so unwelcome.

It is very important to understand this distinction—I am not suggesting that "good things" always happen to people with good attitudes or the opposite. In fact, we often see the opposite and sometimes wonder why God has "blessed" people we might consider "don't deserve it." I suggest, first of all, none of us should be presumptuous and "judge" God's actions. He may be in fact providing us a lesson to learn. Most of us have read more than one story of lottery winners or big-time athletes who received riches most only dream about only to have squandered that abundance and wound up worse and poorer in spirit than when they had nothing. Perhaps they were given the lesson that "abundance" does not necessarily translate into dollars or that having the dollars does not provide one with happiness.

When discussing how the Law of Attraction works, we must sometimes wait even if it seems that we are not getting what we have prayed for or wished to attract.

I will give you an example that happened to me and appeared very contrary to the well-being of me and my family at the time. Although I had asked for a new career in doing what I dreamed of, I still had a job that was paying me well and was providing for us. I should add the pay was no way making us "rich" but at least was able to meet our responsibilities and allows us to be comfortable with our life. It was still, let's say, the pay of a wage earner and not that of an attorney or executive, just good pay for the area we lived in.

Then, and at the time I thought wrongly, I was fired and soon had to take a job paying less than a third of what I had been earning before. It made things suddenly very difficult. But the man who hired me was fair. He was offering me what he could afford and promised me that I would soon earn more once I was there for a while and proved myself on the job. But he also was able to teach me some of the skills I needed to learn to start a business of my own, making the custom furniture I had stated to God and the universe as one of my goals in life. It has come to pass now as indeed God took me from a place where I may have never been able to make the transition and learn the things I needed to succeed and placed me where I needed to be, although it might have not appeared as clear to me at the time.

God will hear our prayers and the things we want to attract, but it is also up to us to trust, to have faith, and to accept. We also may have work to do, and paths to take that at the time may not appear headed where we asked him to take us.

There is a very important distinction I wish to make here because many people who have heard of the Law of Attraction have misunderstood that it indeed is a magnet and not a "wish magnet" in the sense that you will attract like energies and vibrations to those you both consciously and unconsciously put forth, and experience disappointment when the "results" are not what they had "wished for" and thought they were going to attract, then "blame" themselves for their failure. Sadly in our overcommercialized society, there are many who take advantage of many "wishes" people have by promising them "amazing results" with little or no effort on their parts. It might be the come-on ad that offers "lose thirty pounds in six weeks without exercising or changing your diet by taking our fantastic little pill . . ." or "join these amazing folks who became millionaires overnight by just taking our online workshop on . . ." I am quite certain most of us have seen similar offers almost daily; and sometimes we swallow the baited hook and send off our money; and a few weeks later, we not only are in the same or worse shape, but we are also poorer and likely blame either the hucksters, ourselves, or both.

Others will take what I call the "New Year's resolution" path and vow to "do what it takes" to achieve the goal of the resolution. Often, especially down here in Texas and in other areas where the winter climates are relatively mild, we'll see many men and women, usually somewhat overweight or worse, in their new jogging/walking attire, huffing and puffing, that first week or month of the new year. Unwilling to recognize that they did not come to the state they are in a week, month, or frequently a year but often because of a lifestyle for years, they become disenchanted at the hard work and slow results and give up.

I don't mean to pick on only one group of individuals because there are many, those for example who drink or smoke to the detriment of their health and often their families' welfare, others whose finances are a mess, perhaps dissatisfied with jobs or careers in which they feel trapped.

I heard an ad on the radio recently in which two men are talking and one is complaining about not being able to stop smoking. Several times in the brief ad, he states, "I can't" and "I tried" and similar negative expressions of failure to which his friend suggests something he can buy or join, promising him it'll be a breeze to stop.

Think about it—what are you going to attract when you send out the message, "I can't . . ."? A friend says this about "can and can't." "When you say you can't do something, you guarantee you'll succeed at failing to do it. When you say you can, you don't necessarily guarantee success, but you give yourself a chance to succeed at what you want."

Remember this: the Law of Attraction works. It will provide you what you ask for, so if you send out messages of failure, disappointment, fear, blame for either yourself or others, you are sending out vibrations and energies of failure.

Remember this as well: It is not just your conscious energies but your unconscious energies that are being sent out and attracting like energies and results. If you consciously say, "I really want that . . . job, car, whatever result . . ." but subconsciously you have a fear or doubt you are attempting to ignore, your energy and vibrations are mixed signals.

Also, just like the farmer who the other farmer commented about being blessed by God told his friend in so many words, "God helps those who help themselves . . ." You have your own responsibilities in fulfilling the fate you wish to attract.

Accept **your** responsibility but do **not** blame yourself if you have yet to succeed. Remember the saying from our earliest childhood: "If at first you don't succeed, try, try again." There was a very wise successful individual who, when asked about his or her wonderful success, replied something like, "I failed twenty times . . . but I tried twenty-one times!"

Critics of the Law of Attraction often pose the rhetorical question about those starving, in poverty, afflicted by terrible illnesses and similar fates, by derisively asking, "Did they choose to attract their fates?" I cannot honestly answer that other than to think again about how those who do not understand or accept the Law of Attraction are still attracting their fates unconsciously or from a sense of hopelessness. I only know for a fact that in each of these desperate circumstances, there are those who overcome their conditions. Steven Hawking, the British physicist, granted is a genius, but at twenty, he began having symptoms and was diagnosed with a form of ALS and has been confined to a wheelchair for the last half century. Yet this man, who was given only years to live, has continued to astonish physicians and scientists while literally being unable to lift a finger and hardly utter a word. My point is simply that he could have easily fallen into despair at being diagnosed with such a horrible disease but continued to manifest a positive attitude and in turn attracted a very successful future.

Another individual who in this case escaped great poverty came to light recently when he spoke at a presidential prayer breakfast in Washington, DC. Dr. Benjamin Carson is a noted pediatric surgeon who in 2007 was awarded the Presidential Medal of Honor for his accomplishments. During the speech, he spoke of being raised by a single mother, one of twenty-four children, who frequently had to work from early morning until almost midnight! Despite her poverty and only having a third-grade education, she instilled educational values that forever resonated with her son (http://www.theblaze.com/stories/2013/02/08/7-fascinating-facts-about-dr-carson-the-prayer-breakfast-speaker-who-attacked-political-correctness-and-the-debt-in-front-of-obama/).

The common thread in both these anecdotes, which I suggest reveal the positive role of the Law of Attraction, is that neither of these remarkable men or the people in their lives simply accepted their circumstances. Many people, I suggest, live their lives without being aware of the Law of Attraction; and I believe that this ignorance and their simply accepting their sad fates, indeed, "attracts" continuation of their sad and hopeless lives. I suggest when those who criticize the Law of Attraction by stating, "Surely the poor, destitute, starving peoples don't wish to 'attract' their fate" are totally unaware of how their ignorance and sense of helplessness, it brings about or "attracts" their negative without their knowledge. Perhaps those who see this fate that besets these people in poverty, rather than deriding the Law of Attraction, should "use" this awareness to positively attract a better future for these less fortunate rather than sitting idly aside and expressing further negativity. Obviously, there are many missionaries and other well-intentioned individuals and groups who, rather than criticize, volunteer to help the less fortunate. This is not uncommon; in fact, as we have seen, when disaster strikes and assistance is needed, many set aside their own tasks to help, believing that even though each individual's contribution may be small, together they can benefit others. Prayer, faith, and positive energies and vibrations can be sent forth not only from individuals but also from groups of like-minded individuals who seek to attract better circumstances not only for themselves but also for others. The Law of Attraction, indeed, can produce miracles.

We also are all familiar with stories of individuals born to wealth and abundance who have abused themselves and their families and friends, and have in many cases squandered unimaginable riches and circumstances by their actions and energies that have attracted further difficulties into their lives.

There are also others who view people who possess wealth and abundance negatively and with envy, subconsciously expressing a negative association with that wealth and abundance. I ask you how an envious person who both expresses a negative feeling for those with wealth and at the same time consciously covets and wishes similar abundance and wealth for himself will "attract" that wealth when he is essentially sending out negative energies into the universe.

We are all familiar with the verse from 1 Timothy 6:10: *"For the love of money is the root of all evil: which while some coveted after, they have erred from the faith, and pierced themselves through with many sorrows."* In light of the above observation on the envy of wealth and abundance, and the fact that most of us would appreciate more abundance in our own lives, this subject merits a bit more commentary. Although often misquoted as "money is the root of all evil," this verse makes it clear that it is the love or coveting of money, and not the wealth or abundance itself, that is in fact evil or negative. Yes, we have seen greed and evil associated with the rich and powerful, and we have seen not only a status game played by some but also through a media focused on portraying this behavior as entertainment; I feel we do disservice to true goodness, wealth, and abundance. I suggest that the truly abundant and wealthy are also rich in spirit and understand that they can be kind and helpful and assist others. There are two philosophies or "games" as some individuals call the situations. In one "game," which can be illustrated easily in a poker game, if one wins or gains, the other must lose a similar amount. This type of game is called "win-lose" and assumes there is a limited amount of abundance or wealth. The opposite, which I suggest is far more beneficent and realistic as a model of free enterprise, for example, is the "win-win" situation in which one, through positive energies, ideas, and hard work, creates new products and wealth and abundance that is not only a win for him but also a win for everyone who shares that abundance.

I repeat again that whether one accepts it or not, or is ignorant of how the Law of Attraction works, it works for or against people's well-being. I further believe that God and the Bible reveal time and time again that it is God's wish for us to live a good and grateful life, giving service and honor to the Lord and seeking to attract his blessings.

I also suggest that God also "tells" us as to the wisdom of our own wishes, in effect "warning" us in advance that we might be seeking what may not be right for us. Many times we hear of individuals who perhaps are counseled by friends or "hear" the warning from within and choose to ignore the signs perhaps out of pride or fear. "I don't back down . . ." might be a common refrain; another might be, "If it was good enough for my dad, it's good enough for me . . ." and they might maintain the course, despite being on the wrong path.

Sometimes we are also ignorant of the seeds we plant with careless words. "You fool . . ." may be said in frustration and yet hurt another individual without intent. An impressionable child, for example, hearing himself labeled a fool, might unconsciously begin to "attract" lesser states of well-being without the intent or knowledge of the person who foolishly labeled him. Our energies and vibrations can not only attract to us unintended consequences but also harm others, even those we love.

I will add one further example in which one person in a relationship, feeling the other's lack of attention, might express energies and vibrations seeking that attention and love very sincerely. Yet perhaps because the wishes have not been expressed to the other, or have been ignored by the partner, this might result in having the wish expressed for the love and attention, becoming fulfilled by another through illicit means. Sadly, far too many marriages have been damaged and destroyed by one or the other of the partners feeling unloved or unappreciated and, seeking fulfillment of these human needs, have ventured outside the confines of the marriage union. I know of another acquaintance whose wife was everything he could have wished for, was the perfect wife and mother, and he admitted to me that he knew how wonderful she was and how she treated him and the children and yet he couldn't return that love and was driving her away but felt helpless to change. Subconsciously, he was attracting the opposite fate than he should have wished for, for his sake, hers, and the family's. He was "attracting" a manifestation of helplessness. Again, for the Law of Attraction to work for us as God would intend, we must be aligned spiritually with God's spirit and say what we wish to attract without doubt or fear or any conditions attached and have the faith that God will provide us his will.

Regrettably, there are many examples where individuals, loved ones, family members, friends are unaware of how they are truly "attracting" the same fate they fear or wish to avoid by ignoring or otherwise being unaware of or rejecting the Law of Attraction. Just think about it: if a person consistently complains how he hates his job or how unfairly he is treated, or how he's gaining weight or feeling old, and doesn't take active steps to change his circumstances, how are those circumstances going to change? Simply put, if we send out negative energies and vibrations consciously or otherwise, we get back those same negative energies and vibrations and situations.

Therefore, in summary, we must not only understand that the Law of Attraction does work for us all but must also understand we have our own responsibilities in fulfilling the goals we wish to attract. I will also explain later in the guide another important factor in making the Law of Attraction work for us. I believe we must prepare ourselves spiritually to receive and be grateful for the gifts we receive. We will do this by aligning our spirits and energies with God's and believe that with this spiritual centering and trusting of our faith, we can receive the abundance God has intended for us.

NOTES

NOTES

Likewise when the LORD sent you from Kadeshbarnea, saying, Go up and possess the land which I have given you; then ye rebelled against the commandment of the LORD your God, and ye believed him not, nor hearkened to his voice.

Deuteronomy 9 v 23

CHAPTER 3

Why Do Christians Need a Guide?

"Man, alone, has the power to transform his thoughts into physical reality; man, alone, can dream and make his dreams come true."

—*Napoleon Hill*

My reason for writing this guide is to share with others what I have discovered since first learning of the Law of Attraction by watching the movie *The Secret* six years ago. I became convinced that "the secret" or the Law of Attraction was very real in the spiritual sense. I found myself wanting to share with others what I had learned, but when I asked other Christian friends to watch the movie, many of them came back and said, "We watched ten or fifteen minutes, and it's not something Christians should be watching." Although I agree that the movie and many of the writings about the Law of Attraction are very humanistic in their delivery, I believe that one can find this law within the Bible if they know where to search. As I am also a devout Christian, I believe the Bible is God's inspired word. I too believe that God created the earth and everything in it, as well as the moon, the sun, and all the stars in the universe. He also created the laws that govern it, such as the Law of Gravity. I believe that He also created the Law of Attraction and which is as "real" as the Law of Gravity. To this point, I have attempted to explain in the first two chapters what the Law of Attraction is and how it works. Having studied the Bible extensively, I truly believe I can reveal to you that *the secret* is really no "secret" at all but has been right there in the Bible for all Christians to discover and apply to their own lives as God intends us to. I believe God has directed me to write this guide, and I do so to pay honor to him. In the Law of Attraction magazine, there is an article by Neal Donald Walsh, author of *Conversations with God*, where he talks about a lady on Oprah's show. The woman said she and her husband were Christians, and they tried to raise their kids with Christian morals. Her question was, "Where does God fit in with the Law of Attraction?" While I in no way wish to criticize Ms. Byrne nor the others who have written sincerely of the Law of Attraction, I feel this woman's question has not been truly addressed in the way she needs, that is, with specific references found within the Bible. This is why I have written this guide, to give the reader the blueprint one can see and read in their Bible to build their foundation and encourage them to do so.

As I pointed out, while there are skeptics who wish to discount the Law of Attraction, scientists and common people have demonstrated time and time again that it is as much of a universal law as the Law of Gravity. Remember, centuries ago, both the Church of Rome and the scientists of the day stated that the earth was the center of the universe and would burn at the stake those who said otherwise. In their science of the day, America did not exist, and if one sailed to the west from Europe, they would perish by falling off the edge of the earth. Although scientists and even religious and well-meaning people can believe their view of the world and the universe is correct, only God is all-knowing, all-powerful, and the Creator of all. We ignore his laws at our own peril as much now as five hundred years ago.

We must also remind ourselves that although man, through his science and exploration, has now traveled to another heavenly body and keeps probing the atom, his discoveries have only further revealed the glory of God, the Creator. For those of us who have our faith in God's holy word as revealed in the Bible, we know that true science will only continue to shine more light on his creation. We truly have nothing to fear from those who explain the Law of Attraction in humanistic terms because it is they who fail to appreciate how God's laws are there in the Bible for all to discover and benefit from those discoveries. As Jesus told Thomas after he questioned his resurrection, "*Blessed are they who have not seen and yet believe,*" paraphrasing John 20:29.

I also wish to caution you again that as you ignore the Law of Gravity at your own peril, so too do you deny yourselves by ignoring the Law of Attraction, for you are not benefitting fully as you could by following God's laws. Whatever we are experiencing in life, we are attracting it—both positive and negative.

You might say in response, "Hold on a minute, I did not want this negative stuff that's happing to me." I agree you may not consciously want negative things to happen; however, dwelling subconsciously on the negative stuff, as fear and doubt are, in effect attracts negative things into our lives. Remember, it is not only what we consciously wish or pray for, but how we resonate, think, and behave that send forth energies and vibrations into the universe; and these attract the same energies and vibrations back to us. How, for example, will you ever gain prosperity if you always resonate financial lack? Sadly, by feeling with emotion the things we don't want, we end up creating them by default because the Law of Attraction works. If you complain about feeling bad or overweight or you blame yourself or others, your negative energies attract that same result. By failing to understand how the Law of Attraction truly works, we attract by default.

As you learn more about the Law of Attraction, you will learn to direct your thoughts and feelings toward the things that you really want and truly desire. Our universe is made up of physical and nonphysical aspects that are nothing but energy that vibrates. The difference between them is the rate of vibration. Most people think one thing, say another, and then do something else. So what we need to do is get our speech in line with our thoughts, and then our actions will follow that.

I will sum it up this way. The Law of Attraction is the renewing of your mind and putting on the mind of Christ and truly letting the Holy Spirit guide and direct you in everything you do. Many people fail to grasp and make the distinction that we are spiritual beings. God created us as spiritual beings. We are first and foremost a spiritual being experiencing a short-term physical presence in our body. However, if you ask most people what they are, they will answer they are human beings, defining themselves by their physical bodies.

Many of us have a problem distinguishing between the spiritual and the physical. While the Law of Gravity deals with the physical realm that we can see, touch, feel by our physical senses; the Law of Attraction deals with the spiritual realm and therein lies the problem. Just as we "see" and define ourselves as physical beings when in fact we are spiritual, we sometimes fail to appreciate the spiritual laws, which also govern us, connect us to God, our Creator.

This guide is to help people to realize that the God of the Bible created all of the laws that govern our universe. As he created the Law of Gravity, he also created the Law of Attraction. And all of his laws apply equally, whether someone believes in God or not.

I believe the guide will also assist many in overcoming some problems inherent in man's duality as both a physical and spiritual being. God's laws apply to both worlds. The Law of Gravity deals with the physical realm, and the Law of Attraction deals with the spiritual realm. The faithful who centers their spirit with God's learns to hear that still, small voice and understand they are listening to the Holy Spirit. They let him guide them to discover their true purpose in this life.

I know that I am challenging the convictions of many truly faithful Bible-believing Christians in writing this, and I do not wish this to offend or mock you. Rather than write my own opinions, I prefer that this guide use God's words as stated in both the Old and New Testaments for you to follow along in your own Bible. I believe that in doing so, you will discover how the Law of Attraction is revealed time and time again in many ways using many of Jesus's own experiences to provide you the understanding for you to renew your faith and center your spirit. Remember, though, just as with all of God's universal laws, the Law of Attraction applies equally to all people. *For he maketh his sun to rise on the evil and on the good and sendeth rain on the just and on the unjust* (Matt. 5: 45).

As I have pointed out, I have done much research and have read the words of others with regards to the Law of Attraction, humanists, and Christians alike, who have taken different points of view, different approaches in their works. I feel that fellow Christian writer John Place explains the Christian perspective on faith in the following interpretation and wish to credit him for his thoughts. As the Bible provides us the foundation for our faith, I fully agree with his explanation (http://www.johnplaceonline.com/ stress-management/jesus-versus-the-secret-a-christians-guide-to-the-law-of-attraction/).

In discussing the principals of the Law of Attraction, he writes that you must know what you want and believe that you receive it, totally. This is the role of faith. He describes the universe as a mirror, and the Law of Attraction is mirroring back to you your dominant thoughts. I will point out that faith and belief supersede doubt or fear. He writes, "Christianity recognizes the power of faith to bring about positive change, not merely as an internal motivator, but also as an external creative energy."

He goes on to cite the following verses:

Luke 17:6: "*If you have faith as small as a mustard seed, you can say to this tree, Be uprooted and planted in the sea, and it will obey you.*"

Matthew 7:7: "*Ask and ye shall receive.*"

Mark 11:23: "*For verily I say unto you, that whosoever shall say unto this mountain, be thou removed, and be thou cast into the sea; and shall not doubt in his heart, but shall believe that those things which he saith shall come to pass; he shall have whatsoever he saith.*"

He goes on to caution the reader, as I do, that you must align your wishes with God's and not simply consider worldly material possessions as your wish but to also consider your spiritual goals in your understanding of the Law of Attraction and how it works.

> Matthew 13:22: "*The one who received the seed that fell among the thorns is the man who hears the word, but the worries of this life and the deceitfulness of wealth choke it, making it unfruitful.*"

In continuing this a bit further, I will reveal to you how by centering your spiritual self with God's, you will indeed be applying the Law of Attraction as God intended. One of the primary goals of this guide is to encourage and reveal to you how to best renew your Christian spirit.

Think of my guide as a roadmap to help you in this quest. Just as a map guides you to where you want to go, the guide will reveal to you how to center your spiritual being. First, you will learn what truly is the Law of Attraction or, as is stated in the title, God's Law of Attraction. You will read that the Law of Attraction is right in front of you, chapter and verse, so that you can follow along in your Bible. This guide is intended for the faithful as well as the "fence-sitter" or that person who may appreciate the Bible but not yet completely accept it as God's word. Accepting that the Law of Attraction is in line with the teachings of the Bible, you attract the blessings God wishes for you as God provides.

The guide will also provide you cautionary tales to prevent you from misunderstanding or misinterpreting God's will for you. For all our blessings, we are still imperfect beings and therefore may not understand God's greater plan for us. We are still on this earth and know full well that there is pain and suffering as well as goodness and joy.

A Christian accepts that God is perfect, and man is imperfect. God created the universe, the earth, and man by "speaking" it into being; and he gives us the same power over our lives. "*Ask, and it shall be given you; seek, and ye shall find; knock, and it shall be opened unto you*" (Matt. 7:7).

Yet even devout Christians can completely negate their prayers by their unvoiced fears and doubts, negative energy that counters God's wishes for them and attracts that which they fear instead. The guide will demonstrate to you that by not understanding the Law of Attraction as God's law, you bring forth the exact opposite of what you believe you are seeking. By failing to accept and center your spiritual being, you attract the opposite of what God wishes for you. The guide will reveal how, if you follow God's Law of Attraction in your true spirit, you will both prosper and be righteous, for it is God's will.

I believe this guide will reveal to you how to receive the greatest of God's gifts and that by accepting and sharing the blessings you receive from him with others, you will be fulfilling God's wishes for you.

The Bible reveals the glory, power, wisdom, and caring of God. No true Christian doubts this. However, as with many things in our lives, we also must make the effort, take the time, and study carefully to gain the true measure that is contained within the written word. At the risk of being too simple, we can purchase a new camera or phone today, and without carefully reading and understanding the instructions, we may not get all we can from that device. It is true that our lives are very busy with work and family and all our obligations so that we sometimes feel we don't have time to read all the details and instructions. No one will deny this. And, to be honest, sometimes just reading about something does not guarantee that we have fully understood what a camera feature new to us is all about. However, let's say we are with someone who has a more thorough understanding of the camera and is able to point out something we can use and enjoy, it ensures that we will use it for our own pleasure and accomplishment.

In a similar manner, I intend this guide to be a tribute to God and his word by using my years of study of the Bible and the discoveries I have made, combined with the extensive readings of the Law of Attraction I have done over the past five or six years, to take you to the verses in the Bible that demonstrate beyond a doubt that the Law of Attraction is indeed God's law and how you can learn for yourself how the Bible and God intend for you to receive the bounty God wishes for you and also what your responsibilities are to God and to yourself in achieving your dreams.

NOTES

NOTES

The angel of the Lord appeared to him
in a blazing fire from the midst of a bush; and he
looked, and behold, the bush was burning with fire,
yet the bush was not consumed.

Exodus 3 v 2

CHAPTER 4

Who or What Is God?

"You can tell the size of your God by the size of your worry list. The longer the list, the smaller your God."

—Author unknown

In this discussion of God, I wish to point out that I will be focusing entirely on the Christian God as described in the Bible, and I will also assume that the majority of you reading this guide are very aware of the role of faith in identifying God. A friend used an analogy I liked, which he experienced during a drive in the Texas countryside on a sunny morning. The sky was deep blue, and as traffic was light, he allowed himself the luxury of reflecting on how we view the universe and the stars. Granted we all know that the sun is in fact a star, and its brightness combines with the atmosphere to create the beautiful blue skies that we see on sunny days. It is not until the sun sets and the sky becomes dark enough that we begin to see the stars in the night sky. Yet God's universe surrounds us in every direction, but we have never "seen" any of the stars that are out there "during the day"—the sun's light combined with the blue sky prevent this! So when we think about it, we are "trusting" or in fact demonstrating "faith" in the stars that we cannot see. Simply because we cannot see something should never permit us to conclude that it does not exist. Yet there are skeptics who seek exactly that kind of "proof" when they attempt to challenge matters of faith. We do not have to deny our faith or fear because others suggest otherwise.

I also wish to point out that it is not the scope of this guide to prove God's existence. All believers have to have faith. However, the more we know

God and the more we learn about him will result in a stronger faith. The closer our walk is with him, the stronger our faith becomes.

Many cultures and religions over the past millennia have worshiped a supreme deity or group of deities in their daily lives, most often with ceremonies, pomp, and sacrifice and an organized clergy part of their religious practices. Prior to the Christian era, the Greeks and Romans both defined their "gods" by their areas of specialization, the weather, fire, the sea, even love and beauty, where the monotheistic single all-powerful "god" in western culture, at least, is attributed to the Jews and Yahweh. As this guide is intended for Christians and focuses on the Bible, we will limit ourselves to God, the Father, the Son, and the Holy Spirit.

I suggest that in order to know who God is, you have to study his word, the Bible. Here are just some of what the Bible says who God is. I first cite Isaiah 40:12-31, in which the verses enumerate in ways understood to the people of that day that God is the Creator of everything and that he is unequaled.

"[12] *Who hath measured the waters in the hollow of his hand, and meted out heaven with the span, and comprehended the dust of the earth in a measure, and weighed the mountains in scales, and the hills in a balance?*

[13] *Who hath directed the Spirit of the Lord, or being his counsellor hath taught him?*

[14] *With whom took he counsel, and who instructed him, and taught him in the path of judgment, and taught him knowledge, and shewed to him the way of understanding?*

[15] *Behold, the nations are as a drop of a bucket, and are counted as the small dust of the balance: behold, he taketh up the isles as a very little thing.*

[16] *And Lebanon is not sufficient to burn, nor the beasts thereof sufficient for a burnt offering.*

[17] *All nations before him are as nothing; and they are counted to him less than nothing, and vanity.*

[18] *To whom then will ye liken God? or what likeness will ye compare unto him?*

19 *The workman melteth a graven image, and the goldsmith spreadeth it over with gold, and casteth silver chains.*

20 *He that is so impoverished that he hath no oblation chooseth a tree that will not rot; he seeketh unto him a cunning workman to prepare a graven image, that shall not be moved.*

21 *Have ye not known? Have ye not heard? Hath it not been told you from the beginning? Have ye not understood from the foundations of the earth?*

22 *It is he that sitteth upon the circle of the earth, and the inhabitants thereof are as grasshoppers; that stretcheth out the heavens as a curtain, and spreadeth them out as a tent to dwell in:*

23 *That bringeth the princes to nothing; he maketh the judges of the earth as vanity.*

24 *Yea, they shall not be planted; yea, they shall not be sown: yea, their stock shall not take root in the earth: and he shall also blow upon them, and they shall wither, and the whirlwind shall take them away as stubble.*

25 *To whom then will ye liken me, or shall I be equal? saith the Holy One.*

26 *Lift up your eyes on high, and behold who hath created these things, that bringeth out their host by number: he calleth them all by names by the greatness of his might, for that he is strong in power; not one faileth.*

27 *Why sayest thou, O Jacob, and speakest, O Israel, My way is hid from the Lord, and my judgment is passed over from my God?*

28 *Hast thou not known? Hast thou not heard, that the everlasting God, the Lord, the Creator of the ends of the earth, fainteth not, neither is weary? There is no searching of his understanding.*

29 He giveth power to the faint; and to them that have no might he increaseth strength.

[30]Even the youths shall faint and be weary, and the young men shall utterly fall:

[31]But they that wait upon the Lord shall renew their strength; they shall mount up with wings as eagles; they shall run, and not be weary; and they shall walk, and not faint."

I can imagine that if those verses were being written of today's world, they would be written in terms common to us, ensuring that we would understand that all we see, do, are capable of imagining, accomplishing, feeling, sensing, voyaging to the ends of the earth, looking into the very center of the atom, or seeking the edges of his universe, **all is God.**

The Bible indeed tells us God created the universe and all within it. God *is*—we accept this in its full meaning. There was never a time *before* God nor is there space *beyond* God. It is impossible to even *imagine* for even the most skeptical and schooled scientist. Even when they attempt, for example, to describe the beginning of the universe with the "Big Bang" theory, which postulates a moment in which all matter and energy that in their "model" of the universe extends into the infinity of space and calculated by their measurements using the speed at which light travels, in *billions* of years, they cannot answer the one simple question, actually two if you break it down: how did all this energy, mass, time, and space come from *nothing*, and what was there *before* the big bang? These are questions even the most "enlightened" of nonbelievers can answer because they are *incomprehensible*, **beyond** our understanding. We accept the Bible and God as the Creator of all, **forever,** without *beginning* and without *end*. Both Psalm 90:2 and 1 Timothy1:17 attest to God being eternal.

Psalm 90:2: *"Before the mountains were brought forth, or ever thou hadst formed the earth and the world, even from everlasting to everlasting, thou art God."*

1 Timothy 1:17-20: *"[17]Now unto the King eternal, immortal, invisible, the only wise God, be honour and glory forever and ever. Amen.*

[18]This charge I commit unto thee, son Timothy, according to the prophecies which went before on thee, that thou by them mightest war a good warfare;

[19]Holding faith, and a good conscience; which some having put away concerning faith have made shipwreck:

²⁰*Of whom is Hymenaeus and Alexander; whom I have delivered unto Satan, that they may learn not to blaspheme."*

We also accept the biblical account that God created man in his image. Again, there are those who wish to suggest that although they cannot explain the universe without acknowledging God, God had no role in man's "evolution" from single-celled amoebas. They are also stumped, attempting to make the jump from nonliving to living creatures in accounting for the amoebas. They also suggest that this could occur helter-skelter in the universe, which is interesting speculation akin to calculating the number of angels on the head of a pin but in truth placing their "science" at the level of elementary word games.

The Bible describes to us God as walking and talking with Adam and Eve, the first human beings, in the Garden of Eden, in a time before man's original sin. Then God provided Moses the Ten Commandments to teach us how to avoid the sins and wickedness and the temptations of Satan. He is described as so loving his children that he gave us Jesus, his Son, who revealed to man goodness through his actions and miracles and who ultimately died on the cross on Calvary to follow his example and restore our faith and relationship with God. James 4:8: *"Draw nigh to God, and he will draw nigh to you. Cleanse your hands, ye sinners; and purify your hearts, ye double minded."*

God is **All**—all we can individually and collectively touch, taste, see, hear, smell, imagine, and ever know. he is all-powerful. Jeremiah 32:17: *"Ah Lord God! behold, thou hast made the heaven and the earth by thy great power and stretched out arm, and there is nothing too hard for thee."* He is all-knowing, in all things, in all places, without limit as in 1 Kings 8: 27: *"But will God indeed dwell on the earth? Behold, the heaven and heaven of heavens cannot contain thee; how much less this house that I have builded?"* He is without limits, as in Jeremiah 23:24: *"'Can any hide himself in secret places that I shall not see him?' saith the Lord. 'Do not I fill heaven and earth?' saith the Lord."* God **exists** at all times—past, present, and future—and in all our spirits as love. We simply *cannot* conceptualize *nothing*, a *nonexistence;* it is impossible.

As such, God is within us all as God exists beyond the physical universe, although he can create and destroy at will in the physical realm, God is spiritual, in our minds, hearts, and souls.

We human beings think in terms of either black or white, hot or cold, good or bad, to name a few. God's universe can be described as encompassing all, the ever-changing and the constant, the physical and the spiritual. Yet God's moral character does not evolve with the times but remains constant. God is perfection, all-knowing.

Yet above all, as stated so simply in 1 John 4:8: *"He that loveth not knoweth not God; for God is love."* All twenty-one verses in 1 John 4 attest to

God's being all-loving. Perhaps one of the most eloquently stated truths can be summed up in the statement that to know love is to know God, and if we open our eyes to the beauty of God's creations, we can experience this daily. Not only do we mean the love of Valentine's, the love between a man and a woman, but between child and parent, between an owner and his or her pet, between friends, even how we may feel about the love of the beauty around us, the skies, the seas, the animals, and the plants in God's natural world. The more we love, the more we see more to love, and we experience God's love for us just as we love him. In its simplest and most profound sense, this is perhaps the greatest evidence of the Law of Attraction, that as we send forth love, we so receive God's love in return.

There are also truths of God that we must know on faith. Although God is said to live in heaven, we as imperfect beings do not possess the ability to truly "see" heaven, although we are told that if we are found righteous on the Day of Judgment, then we will enter heaven, the throne room of God's kingdom. Until that time, we must live our lives in the faith that God is indeed everywhere, both in the physical and spiritual universes.

As we have been told that we as human beings have been created in the Image of God, we have seen many times God depicted in the human form, usually as a man, although both men and women were both created in his image. In Genesis 1: 27: "*So God created man in his own image, in the image of God created he him; male and female created he them.*" Perhaps we might also consider that the Bible says God is a spirit (John 4:24: "God is a Spirit: and they that worship him must worship him in spirit and in truth")—beyond physical form; and when the righteous among us join him in the kingdom of God, we will indeed see him as he is (1 John 3:2: "Beloved, now are we the sons of God, and it doth not yet appear what we shall be: but we know that, when he shall appear, we shall be like him; for we shall see him as he is") and be like him, possessing spiritual bodies (1 Cor. 15:44: "It is sown a natural body; it is raised a spiritual body. There is a natural body, and there is a spiritual body").

We know that in Genesis, God walked with Adam and Eve and that the paradise he created was perfect. However, through their failure to follow God's instructions, Adam and Eve fell from grace; and from that moment until now, man's imperfection has created many trials and tribulations, famines, wars, hunger, greed, lust, anger. Although God was offended by the licentious behavior of those who sinned and did on occasion punish them, he offered man the Ten Commandments for him to follow and to be found righteous on the Day of Judgment.

Yet the greatest evidence of God's love and hope for mankind was in sending his Son to be born and to Live and die among mankind. John

3:16: "For God so loved the world, that he gave his only begotten Son, that whosoever believeth in him should not perish, but have everlasting life." It would have been right and proper for Jesus to have been born of nobility in the most elegant of earthly kingdoms, but that was not God's purpose in sending forth his Son.

No one can truly challenge the statement that the birth, life, and crucifixion of Jesus of Nazareth marked the most significant turning point in human history. Although God exists always, Jesus his Son was born in a humble stable to Mary and Joseph, in Bethlehem of Judea. Jesus grew up to be a man, taught throughout Palestine, and performed miracles to reveal his divinity. Yet as we have seen countless times through history, evil people existed; and in many cases, they held high and holy office and were threatened by the presence and teachings of Jesus, fearing their own religious hypocrisy would be exposed. They felt their only solution was to conspire, falsely accuse him of treason, and bring him to trial so that he may legally be put to death. Jesus was tortured and crucified in the cruelest of deaths, nailed by his hands and feet to a wooden cross to slowly suffer before eventually perishing. Many mocked him, suggesting that if he were indeed the Son of God, he would not die in this manner, that God would spare him his suffering. However, on the third day following his crucifixion, Jesus rose from the dead and, in the time that followed, was seen by hundreds of people who bore witness to the fact that the Son of God had indeed lived among them and, although executed, had continued to live, revealing his holiness. Jesus then instructed his followers to *go and make disciples of all nations, baptizing them in the name of the Father and of the Son and of the Holy Ghost* (Matt. 28:19). And thus the world has Christianity, which his disciples and followers have taken throughout the world.

As Christians, we are provided the Bible, which is God's word, divided into both the Old Testament, written of the times from the Creation of the universe and earth to the birth of Christ, and the New Testament, which moves forward from his birth to the end of times.

As a devout Christian who fully accepts the Bible as the word of God, I nonetheless do not claim to understand God as I might another person, any more than I can, in my physical being, grasp the idea of a universe that extends infinitely or an existence beyond time. No, I do not write this skeptically but wish to convey my limitations as a human being on this physical plane called the earth. I have studied and continue to study daily my Bible; and I believe I accept that it is not my destiny on this earth, nor anyone else's for that matter, to be able to extend myself into God's being, except through sharing my faith and my love and recognizing my humble duty not only to myself and my loved ones but also to others. In this way, I hope to reveal my faith and gratitude and at the time of judgment be judged as worthy.

I hope that my devotion to the Bible and the commandments of God has enabled me to not only embrace God through faith but also to feel joy and thanksgiving knowing he is within me.

Extending this thought forward and reflecting again on the Bible and the book of Genesis and how God walked with Adam and Eve, I wish to suggest that we all consider God not only as all-knowing and all-powerful but also as a friend who walks with us and gives strength of spirit to be our best, to express the love we know to be the manifestation of God and his greatest gift, and to seek to do his will. There are times all of us, in times of hardship and travail, need the encouragement and support of a friend, and I suggest the truest friend we all can know is God. God offers intimate and lasting friendship to those who reverence him (Ps. 25:14: "The secret of the Lord is with them that fear him; and he will shew them his covenant"). What relationship could ever compare with having the Lord of all creation for a friend? Your everlasting friendship with God will grow as you reverence him. Our faith gives us that knowledge that the best friend in the universe is within us.

NOTES

NOTES

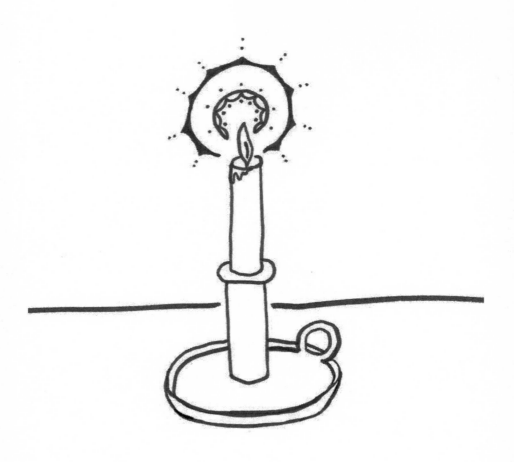

So God created man in his own image,
in the image of God created he him;
male and female created he them.

Genesis 1 v 27

CHAPTER 5

Who or What Is Man?

"Gratitude is an attitude that hooks us up to our source of supply. And the more grateful you are, the closer you become to your maker, to the architect of the universe, to the spiritual core of your being. It's a phenomenal lesson."

—*Bob Proctor*

This question has been asked since the dawn of time, and there are as many views and answers as there are cultures and people responding. One could easily fill a number of books reviewing these frequently divergent points of view so I will attempt to simply provide a brief overview before providing you the answer I believe the Bible provides.

In his introduction, the author cited below states, "With reference only to our biology we can say that we are carbon-based life-forms that have self-awareness" (http://glory2godforallthings.com/2012/05/30/what-is-man/). He is not supporting this thesis so much as simply stating the fact that often scientists in their research attempt to concentrate on the physical without regard to the spiritual, which is their discipline, but their scholarship in no way can disprove a fact they choose to ignore.

Descartes, in the seventeen hundreds, provided a simple answer—*I think therefore I am*—which in many ways holds a very basic truth about man. He is different from the animals in that he has the ability to think, listen to his inner conscience, and control to some degree his condition in the world. Humans alone can sense God's wonder and communicate that to others; and others, in turn, can decide for themselves how to conduct their own lives.

Continuing, the Preamble to the American Declaration of Independence reads: "We hold these truths to be self-evident that all men are created equal, that they are endowed by their Creator with certain inalienable Rights, that among these are Life, Liberty and the pursuit of Happiness." The Preamble is based on the account of creation of man revealed in the Genesis, believed to be the word of God. Empirical observation, however, reveals that men are not created equal, either physically or mentally; and the Bible does not explain the inequalities and differences in inheritance of genes, complexion, gender, nationality, congenital handicaps or retardation, the initial circumstances in the formative and impressionable years of life, etc. (http://www.hknet.org.nz/GP-OriginOfMan-RSP.html). Again, the scientist practices hubris, assuming that his "observation" of physical inequalities disproves or undermines the spiritual content of the Preamble.

Yet it is easy to believe that most agree to certain basic principles such as those stated in the Preamble above, but even that is misleading. While here in our country, we have grown comfortable to seeing women as attorneys, doctors, even airline pilots, in some Muslim nations, women are not permitted to drive.

I will touch on this later, but let me conclude that we could continue to survey many different cultural and philosophical differences without reaching any compromise, and this is not the point of this guide anyway.

The Christian accepts the definition that the Bible provides, that man is created in the likeness and image of God. As we believe that God became man through the birth and life of Jesus Christ, we also attribute many values as to man's rights, which others refer to frequently as human rights. If one takes this position that human rights arises from the idea of human dignity, which rests on the belief that man was created in the image and likeness of God, we confirm the spiritual value that forms the bedrock of the transcendent rights of man. If we fail to consider God's relationship to man and only acknowledge man's ability to think and function differently from all other beings, we provide leaders with different values the excuse to be nothing more than a more intelligent life form, a dangerous threat to God's creation. Otherwise, the culture of man is based not on fundamental values but on the power of the state, which is the creation of man and represent only the current political climate of that nation and time.

One need only consider a number of the most tragic examples of power-based states in the twentieth century—Nazi Germany, the Soviet Union, mainland China, and even the Pol Pot regime in Cambodia—to conclude that secular states divorced from a spiritual center such as the Bible can and have killed millions to maintain their corrupt states. For the concepts of individual rights, human dignity, and respect for others, there has to be a strong underpinning of spiritual values upon which those rights remain anchored, beyond the power of the individual leaders.

If one accepts that man is created in the image of God, that endows human beings with divine spiritual values that endow that person with God's worth. Our rights therefore empower each human life, every person, with dignity that the state cannot remove. In other words, we must as Christians hold to these values as coming from God and not just one of many assertions answering the question what is man?

Yet these assertions of various human rights in the west, when heard by some nonwestern cultures, do not sound like truth claims, only like cultural imperialism. Should women be allowed to drive cars in Saudi Arabia? The answer depends solely on who is speaking. Obviously, many nations have distorted this basic premise to provide greater rights to certain persons. Medieval kings, through their power over their dominions and control over the state apparatus, often coerced their religious hierarchies to confirm that the nobility had greater rights and that the king's rights were conferred by God.

There is much confusion in modern man as well because so much of the contemporary culture, the industry, the educational establishment, the political life, and the contemporary life in general avoids dealing with answering "Who or what is man?" in the spiritual context, despite the fact that man's presence on this earth, created in the image and likeness of God, logically must also have a definite relationship to God the Creator's purpose for man.

For Christians whose faith is anchored in the Bible, all human beings exist in the image of God, and none can be more or less in that image than any other. We accept the truth that Christ was that image in human form, and being God, he confirms that our rights and dignity as human beings are spiritually based and inviolate. John 3:16: "For God so loved the world, that he gave his only begotten Son, that whosoever believeth in him should not perish, but have everlasting life."

If we acknowledge the Bible's affirmation that man was created in the image and likeness of God, and further believe that God created all and is perfect, and accept man's imperfection resulting from his original sin, we can both understand man's difficulties, strife, wars, plague, and pestilence over the millennia. No matter how man strives to achieve wealth, happiness, well-being, and such apart from God, he is doomed to fall short. Romans 3:23: "For all have sinned, and come short of the glory of God."

In discussing the Law of Attraction without first centering oneself spiritually, one falls victim to the above scripture. Again, the question is perfectly posed in Matthew 16:26: "For what is a man profited, if he shall gain the whole world, and lose his own soul? or what shall a man give in exchange for his soul?" Man cannot gain the kingdom of heaven nor truly experience the abundance God has in store for him without first accepting Christ as his Savior and aligning himself spiritually with God. John 14:6: "Jesus saith unto him, 'I am the way, the truth, and the life: no man cometh unto the Father, but by me.'"

As this guide focuses on the Law of Attraction being a law of God's based in the Bible, we have other questions that we should examine as even we as Christians hold different views on what God intends for us, some suggesting that rather than abundance, he is pleased by those living a life of poverty, or on the other extreme, some living lives of extravagance, excessive material possessions, and consumption.

I feel that there is ample evidence in the Bible that God intends us to have abundance. However, there are some cautions that one should exercise in understanding this better. There are those who prosper financially and enjoy the apparent blessings of abundance because they are adhering to the laws of attraction, but in the spiritual sense, they are not enjoying the true abundance that God promises those who believe in his word. I suggest that this might be the main weakness with *The Secret*, which presents the Law of Attraction with less grounding in its spiritual nature, suggesting that the energy that one voices and that does attract like vibrations in return is in and of itself sufficient. While there is ample evidence that does reveal that individuals can attract good fortune in the material sense, there are far too many cases that gaining that goal, that wealth, or that object does not truly satisfy their inner selves or in truth their spiritual self. I feel that if they first center themselves spiritually, and then "enlist" God's wishes for them, their gains will be consistent with what God intends for them. I will explore this further in the chapter on renewing our faith.

I also believe that while God intends abundance for us, that this need not be necessarily extreme abundance or excessive wealth. I think of the individual who is reputed to own a dozen Rolls-Royces, Bentleys, and other luxury cars. Yet in his nation, his people live in extreme poverty. Perhaps this is one of the most extreme cases of profligation that one can cite; nonetheless, one should not equate excessive material possessions with one's quality as a human being and spiritual follower of Christ. Mark 8:36: "For what shall it profit a man, if he shall gain the whole world, and lose his own soul?" Our popular culture and entertainment inundates us daily with extreme examples of material wealth and excess, prompting envy, insecurity, and greed, suggesting to those who are without strong spiritual anchors that these are examples of success, as though the material blessings these individuals have received provide them greater happiness and well-being, when we often see those same individuals admitting to drug abuse, broken marriages, and unhappiness. I do not wish this to say that people should not seek abundance, and some will in fact prosper greatly, while others less so; but those who find true happiness and abundance are the ones whose spiritual center and soul are safe within God's wishes and protection, not those who sacrifice their souls for material gains.

Although man was created in the image and likeness of God, man separated himself from being godlike through his original sin. Therefore, man cannot understand God's plan other than through the Bible and fails whenever he acts or assumes to rise to the level of God, either through claiming godlike wisdom or knowledge. God did provide him stewardship over his earthly domain. He must use his knowledge and his spirituality to serve God and, in that service, also serve man and nature. Time and again, we have seen examples of how man's ignorance, greed, and excessive pride have blinded him to this. In a sense, the lesson of the tower of Babel prepares us for this. Man believed he could construct a tower to reach the heavens and rise to the level of God, only to fail. But we see this repeatedly in today's world as well. Man has abused his natural world and environment, either in stripping productive land and turning it to dust, or by polluting the land and streams and lakes, an environment intended by God to provide us abundance through bountiful harvests and natural beauty. Sadly, this is often not done by the ignorant so much as by those who ignore God and his natural creations.

In the beginning, God did walk with Adam in the garden; but because of Adam and Eve's sin, there was a period between this time and the Coming of Christ, when man's only way to reach God was through the priests and prophets. However, with the birth of Christ, God walked among men, and they knew the presence of God *in the flesh!* Man was again able to know God and feel his Presence. They were able to hear his words, see his miracles, and understand God's kingdom firsthand. As his coming had been prophesized, the Israelites had eagerly anticipated God's kingdom as an earthy one for his chosen people. However, with the birth of Christ, the kingdom of God had come; but it was for his faithful everywhere, and it was a kingdom not of golden thrones but a spiritual kingdom for those who believed and followed him.

Yet it is important to understand how we should view God and his Son Jesus. How should we view him in the manger as a newborn Jesus? Or perhaps as the gentle preacher who suggested turning the other cheek? Or crucified on the cross, suffering for us?

I suggest it is our responsibility to see Jesus for what he is, God the Son, on the throne with his Father, wearing his crown. For if we do not attribute the reality of his being God in the magnificence of heaven, we do not grasp the importance of his earthly presence as it should be seen. For God again walked with man and gave man the opportunity to be in his presence, God's presence.

Let us consider a bit more how man ignores his relationship to God, not only through those we might view as unlearned but also the opposite, those who consider their knowledge capable of providing them godlike powers, false wisdom, enabling them to feel they can exercise authority over man and nature without considering the consequences of their hubris.

I found it of interest to read some observations of a French scholar who visited America in the early nineteenth century and became an ardent champion of America's democratic freedoms, writing two books on the subject. He was a man who without pride or hesitation acknowledged his faith in God (http://en.wikipedia.org/wiki/Alexis de Tocqueville). I cite a couple of his observations because they are very wise and applicable even a hundred and seventy-five years later. "I am unaware of his plans but I shall never stop believing in them because I cannot fathom them and I prefer to mistrust my own intellectual capacities than his justice." I believe that if more people acted in accordance with this statement of faith rather than believing their own intellect superior, we might be in a better place today. On the political side, he wrote this simple eloquent view of our democracy: "Liberty cannot be established without morality, nor morality without faith." I suggest that in considering the term "morality" in this context, it would be the morality God instills in us and provides us through the Bible, respecting others and treating them with respect, honor, and justice rather than with the false morality of acting as judge of others, allowing God to pass judgment as is his power and not ours. In this final quote, de Tocqueville champions democracy and limited authority in this observation: "As I see it, only God can be all-powerful without danger, because his wisdom and justice are always equal to his power. Thus there is no authority on earth so inherently worthy of respect, or invested with a right so sacred, that I would want to let it act without oversight or rule without impediment." You might find other observations of his enjoyable to read at this site: http://www.goodreads.com/work/quotes/90454-de-la-d-mocratie-en-am-rique.

There are those men and women who through the ages have viewed science and knowledge as contradictory to the teachings of the Bible and antithetical to God and faith. Yet I suggest it is perfectly within God's plan, for he created man and in doing so also gave man the ability to progress in technology as a means of improving his stewardship over the earth. Using his role as steward, man was to improve the physical earth as God gave it to him, continuing its creation and, in so doing, serving as a testament to God's way of life. Furthermore, in this very process of continuing the creation and attesting to God's holy, righteous character, man would live in accordance with God's instructions. However, man was tempted by Satan in the garden, and in violating God's warning, man committed the original sin and revealed himself to be imperfect and had to then rely on his own choices how to conduct his life on this earth.

Despite God's displeasure with man's violation of his warning, God gave man his spiritual side to act in balance with his knowledge and expanding discoveries about the world around him. I suggest that properly applied, these discoveries were to improve man's life here on earth as well as provide him more abundance in accordance with his plan. We must also acknowledge that although our knowledge and research have provided us progress in certain areas, we have also lost knowledge through our own advances, often discrediting the ways of old in favor of the untested new ways. Today we have overwhelming evidence of this all around us—our diets, that once was based on whole foods with natural nutrients from the earth, became the subject of "scientific improvements," which have led to artificial ingredients, processed foods, and a plethora of increasing health-related problems that have very negatively affected our quality of life. We can see allergies, obesity, and physical ailments such as cancer and heart disease, which I suggest have resulted from our being led astray by those whose faith in our "scientific developments," triumphed over our spiritual faith and resulted in these true plagues of modern life.

Sadly, too many have ignored their spiritual self, focusing instead only on their life here on earth and their misplaced faith in man. For centuries, man has even pursued his knowledge in many cases to "disprove" God, only to fail miserably. Even when he seeks to "prove" God, he is acting foolishly, spending his limited time on this planet, seeking answers to questions only God will reveal the answer at a time in the future when the chosen reside with him in heaven.

This is not to suggest that those who champion a materialistic, man-driven universe with knowledge and science ignoring faith and spirituality have in any way surrendered their wish to direct us toward their vision of an earthly paradise as though that were possible. More and more, they have risen to power within today's society. In a sense, the technology that has grown exponentially to invade all areas of our lives has provided "data" and information that these learned ones seek to employ to "define" us mathematically. To them, as well as to those who label themselves the scientists, nothing exists if it cannot be measured and quantified. Many among us "know the price of everything and the value of nothing."

We can also see darker possible applications of man's disregard for God's goodness in the purposes for his research. Either through ignorance or worse purposeful disregard or malevolence, we might suspect the "mapping of the brain" as a means of seeking control over the individual's brain, whether for curative reasons or otherwise. We can look at the field of genetic engineering as it applies to agriculture and leave with little confidence in man's ability to interfere with nature's processes. While the stated goal is to "improve" crop yield and enable the plants to be genetically engineered to combat invasive organisms, there are those who have research revealing the possibility that these "improvements" can actually be harmful to man, despite the proponents' claims otherwise. The GMO question, which in our country still is in debate, has been soundly rejected in numerous countries who feel that Mother Nature is a better provider for us than a group of ambitious, arrogant scientists and researchers seeking enormous profits.

Perhaps these two humorous examples of "intellectual logic" and common sense might be a good fit here. Zeno was a Greek philosopher who lived in the fifth century before Christ. He provided a paradox that still today "proves" that in a race between a tortoise and a hare, for example, the hare can never win . . . *if* the tortoise is given a head start. This is more a mathematical challenge than the tortoise-hare example more common to us, in which the hare loses because of his laziness and cockiness. In Zeno's paradox, let's say the tortoise, because it can "run" only one-tenth the speed of the hare, is given a fifty-yard head start. In the time the hare runs the fifty yards, the tortoise moves ahead another five yards. In the time the hare runs those five yards, the tortoise moves ahead another half yard, so on and so forth. This is amusing because although we all know that the hare would zoom ahead through "commonsense" mathematical proof of the kind, most of us are used to "proving" the tortoise never being overtaken by the hare. Essentially, man, through his sophistry and intellectual capacity, can often misdirect both his inquiries and his choices from simple, wise ones to focusing and debating nonsensically. Faith does not require debating with anyone, simply following one's own spiritual beliefs. The time when all questions will be answered is not yet at hand.

A second example of this in the form of a tale from the past involves two horse riders who must race across the desert from one town to another. However, the contest involves a twist, as the two riders are told, "The rider whose horse **arrives second** will be rewarded with great riches." The two riders mount their horses and race off into the desert, but as they draw near to the other town, they have begun to slow, neither wishing to arrive first. Then, finally, a short distance from the town, they both literally stop, and neither advances. They both grow weary in the sun and heat and are on the verge of collapse, when a stranger approaches and asks why they are stranded in the desert so near the town, literally in danger for their lives. The men disclose the terms of the contest, to which the stranger reflects a moment and tells them both something. Suddenly, both riders mount the horses and race off as fast as they can ride. The question is, "What did the man tell the riders?" The answer: "Why don't you get on each other's horse?"

I believe that many intellectuals, scientists, and other "learned" individuals also can be guilty of ignoring simple wisdom and get locked into their views or logical beliefs, thereby failing to take into consideration common sense when closely examined. Of course, very often those calling the *intelligentsia* or other authorities into question are ignored or worse vilified for defying them. The powers that be, the authorities, the "system" that includes virtually all of our daily matrix of living, frequently calling into question and marginalizing those who question their "rules"—perhaps they should be held more accountable for their ignoring their spiritual values or attempting to make us act in ways in conflict with ours. Matthew 11:25: "At that time Jesus answered and said, I thank thee, O Father, Lord of heaven and earth, because thou hast hid these things from the wise and prudent, and hast revealed them unto babes." Often we have heard the phrase "Out of the mouths of babes . . . ," suggesting insights and wisdom coming from those most innocent and least "experienced" by education.

Whether in politics, the arts, or popular culture, there are many who are swayed by the current fashion or trend and are either swept along, suggesting they are "progressive" in their thinking and actions, criticizing or dismissing those who suggest otherwise. However, if one has taken the wrong road and fails to turn back, by continuing down that road in a mistaken direction, are they in fact "progressing" toward their goals?

Because man cannot "prove" God through his limited imperfect being, what is left? I suggest that the answer is faith and that this is perhaps the simplest of decisions one has to make in his life. Leave the endless debates to those who choose ignorance over enlightenment through faith. Rather than seeking answers to the unanswerable, let them open their eyes on a starry night and behold the wonders of God's universe or walk along a stream in a forest or a flower garden and rejoice in the beauty of nature, or marvel at the magic of the human brain, all God's creations, which reveal God all around us and reveal why our lives on earth are far better spent seeking harmony in faith with his Spirit.

Therefore, I suggest the answer to the question of who or what is man is best answered by stating that above all, man is a spiritual being here on earth for a finite time and that his ultimate relationship with God is based on faith.

I wish to go back, in closing this chapter, to offering a personal observation in regard to how we view Jesus. I ask that you each consider this very carefully because I suggest that understanding and viewing Jesus as sitting in heaven with the Father provide man the awareness to truly appreciate, in the lyrics of that famous hymn, "what a friend we have in Jesus." There are times in each of our lives when understanding that we can indeed be with Jesus and that he is not only God but also our friend, and that we truly appreciate the meaning of this spiritually, allows us the gift of his love and strength at times, which otherwise can be so difficult for us to accept. One day during the most recent Christmas season, I got a call from my son informing me that his brother had accidentally shot himself in the head. His mother and I did not have any further information as to his condition, and she hurriedly left the next morning to be at his side. I truly do not know how, without knowing that Jesus was at my side giving me the strength and love to know everything was in God's hands, I don't know how I could have fared during those horrible hours. As it turned out, he survived and was miraculously spared brain damage. He has recovered with nothing but scars. Praise God.

I know that those of you who have the same faith in your relationship with Jesus know my sense of gratitude, and I offer to each of you the counsel that you each examine how you truly see Jesus and his presence in your lives.

NOTES

NOTES

In the beginning God created
the heaven and the earth.

Genesis 1 v 1

CHAPTER 6

How God Made the Earth and Everything in It

"In the beginning God created the heaven and the earth."

—*Genesis 1:1*

According to the Bible, Genesis 1 describes how God made the earth and everything in it. **"¹In the beginning God created the heaven and the earth."** On that first day, he also created light. *"³And God said, 'Let there be light' and there was light."* However, he did not create the sun, moon, and stars until the fourth day (verses 14-19). My question to you is where did the light come from on the first day? I offer you this answer: his glory!

Let us continue with the creation of the earth and the universe as we will be able to see his plan for man. On the third day, he created the plants, grass, and trees as well as the land and seas. *"¹⁰And God called the dry land earth; and the gathering together of the waters called the seas: and God saw that it was good. ¹¹And God said, 'Let the earth bring forth grass, the herb yielding seed, and the fruit tree yielding fruit after his kind, whose seed is in itself, upon the earth': and it was so."*

After giving us the sun for light during the day and the stars for lesser light in the darkness of night, and plant life to sustain the animal life on the earth, he then continued his creation the fifth day. *"²¹And God created great whales, and every living creature that moveth, which the waters brought forth abundantly, after their kind, and every winged fowl after his kind: and God saw that it was good.* ²²And *God blessed them, saying, 'Be fruitful, and multiply, and fill the waters in the seas, and let fowl multiply in the earth.'"*

So by the sixth day, the earth was ready for man. "²⁶*And God said, 'Let us make man in our image, after our likeness: and let them have dominion over the fish of the sea, and over the fowl of the air, and over the cattle, and over all the earth, and over every creeping thing that creepeth upon the earth.' ²⁷So God created man in his own image, in the image of God created he him; male and female created he them."*

He created man in his own image and gave man dominion over all his other creations on this earth. In this order of creation, he had prepared an earthly paradise for those he created in his image to live in abundance and prosper. And we know, God created the earth for our pleasure and prosperity by taking a moment to savor his creation in the wonderful taste of a piece of fruit or offer a rose to your love or gaze into the heavens and feel the joy and serenity of his creation, or behold a newborn child and see the pure love in the eyes of the mother and father. Sometimes in the haste and distraction of the modern world, we need to pause and renew our appreciation for his creation of this earth and all within it.

It is important to recall a central point to all of this creation.

He created the world in preparation for man. He also gave man the stewardship over all he created on the earth. Along with man's stewardship over all God created, man was given the same power over our lives to create also by our thoughts and words.

As the Bible states in Genesis 1:3: "God said, 'Let there be light' and there was light."

What did God use to create everything in the world? I believe he spoke everything into being. What does the scripture say? It says:

> Hebrews 11:3: "Through faith we understand that the worlds were framed by the word of God, so that things which are seen were not made of things which do appear."

> John 1:1-3:

> "¹In the beginning was the Word, and the Word was with God, and the Word was God.

> ²The same was in the beginning with God.

> ³All things were made by him; and without him was not anything made that was made."

I feel it necessary to emphasize the power of the spoken word and how, both in the Old Testament and the New Testament, we read how powerful the word is. 1 Peter 1:25: "But the word of the Lord endureth for ever. And this is the word which by the gospel is preached unto you."

This power God manifested is also provided to us, so that we not only believe our faith but also speak our faith. Earlier, in chapter 3, I used the following as an example to illustrate this:

> Mark 11:23: "For verily I say unto you, that whosoever shall *say* unto this mountain, be thou removed, and be thou cast into the sea; and shall not doubt in his heart, but shall *believe* that those things which he *saith* shall come to pass; he shall have whatsoever he *saith*."

It is important to note that while the belief, the faith, appears once in the above verse, three times the spoken word is employed. Paraphrasing the final sentence—the things we say will come to pass—we will have whatever we say.

For the Law of Attraction to work, we must ask or speak those wishes to God and the universe. I suggest for the Christian whose faith is anchored in the Bible, it was often difficult when *The Secret* appeared to not consider it as humanistic, new age, because rarely was God given credit for his power and love in the original book. I have already pointed out as well that simply "wishing" something materialistic would not necessarily bring the gratification that one had imagined. Many of us have experienced the longing for something without thinking it through, believing that the "thing" we sought would bring us happiness, only to discover that we felt largely the same as before we received it. So one truly must imagine the thing that he wishes and then ask himself if it is just the material possession that he wishes or if he truly has considered his spiritual side in the wish. I point out that I am speaking to the devoted Christian who seeks to lead a spiritual life and follow the spirit of the Bible and the word of God, not just the person who claims Christianity to appear on Sunday at services but not live his life in accordance with the Bible otherwise. I am not passing judgment nor asking you to pass judgment, for we can only look into our own hearts and not enter the hearts and minds of others. But I do suggest that if we do not align our spirits with Christ and truly understand the biblical Law of Attraction as it appears therein, we do not attract the true bounty that God can provide us. But in addition to asking ourselves and feeling we are in line with our spiritual selves, we must speak, say to the universe, that which we wish to receive. There is the story of Christians after the Judgment Day who are walking around in heaven and seeing a building where people are entering and leaving. They see that the people leaving appear to be saddened. When they ask about, wanting to see for themselves what is inside the building, their guide cautions them; but after they keep asking, he tells them that each person's "file" is within, and the people are allowed to read their files. When one of the persons asks why they appear so sad, he is told how the folders contain what God had intended for the person, but they had never asked for these blessings. Sadly, we may deny ourselves the blessings of abundance by simply being ignorant of the Law of Attraction and seeking these blessings from God, asking for them.

It should be of interest when discussing the Law of Attraction, the role of faith, and the world of scientific research, which many view as hostile and contrary to one's faith, that even scientific skeptics are finding that science itself is reinforcing the role of positive energy and thoughts from one's mind as having measurable results confirmed by purely mechanical scientific devices. Here, a noted scientist discusses the research conducted and the results (http://vimeo.com/4359545).

This leads into the next point of this, which involves how we do in fact create our own world, in a similar manner to how God created the earth. As the Law of Attraction is in fact a spiritual law of God's, it works for us in creating our world, whether we understand this or not. Ignorance of this law does not mean we will not attract the fate we "speak" and send out to the universe. How many people have you heard whose first word is negative, how something is wrong in their lives? They might be paupers or they might be people of wealth, but as they voice their complaints, they send forth negative energies into the universe, and they do attract negative returns, compounding their negativity. While they might claim to do all within their power to improve their lives, they are speaking negative energies and negative wishes, and their lives do not achieve the improvement they claim to wish consciously. "I'll never be able to stop smoking" is no way to stop smoking; "I'd love that job, but I'm sure someone else is already picked out and this is all a charade" does not attract that job into your future.

I have already written this point before, but I wish to emphasize it because I feel it is fundamental to understanding the Law of Attraction. That is, the Law of Attraction not only involves the thoughts and conscious energies, wishes, and vibrations you "choose" to express but the unconscious or subconscious ones as well. Perhaps this example will illustrate the point. You are in the middle of writing a message on your computer, which is a conscious expression on your part. For this example, you are using an older computer, which is plugged into the wall. Out of the blue, the electricity goes off, even for a second or two, and when it comes back on, all your message is gone, lost! Or instead of hitting the save or send button, you hit delete. I think most of us have experienced something like this.

Now imagine that consciously, daily, you have been seeking to attract something you sincerely want for yourself into your future; and you feel that it is something that God and the universe would wish for you to have. But let's just suggest that somewhere in your unconscious or even in your conscious, there is this little "impulse" of apprehension, doubt, fear, a negative energy. Now imagine the first moment when you wake up, you feel this impulse expressed, somehow you have concern or anxiety, and that negative energy is released. Bang! You have in effect "erased" your message, all the work you consciously had expressed for yourself and your wish.

I don't wish this to offend you, but I will give you a different scene when you wake up. For example, as you sense the daylight, your first impulse is not, "Whew, the sun made it this morning!" In both your conscious and your unconscious mind, you have absolutely no doubt that the sun's light will be shining on you as it did yesterday and will tomorrow. This is a subtle point; yes, we "know" the sun rises in the morning, and it does daily. But as human beings, in fact, we do not have the "power" to *know* the future, but we have literally *total faith* in the future, certainly as far as the sunrise or that the flowers will blossom in the spring. Obviously, the latter example can be affected by the amount of rain we have had, other "natural" changes within God's earth, but we "know" the future because of our "faith" in the future.

In an upcoming chapter on renewing your faith, we will go into this in greater detail, and I will show you how to truly center yourself spiritually so that your conscious and your unconscious spirit are aligned with your faith in God and that you won't have these little "bursts" of unconscious negative energies that work against yourself. We all know that faith provides us wonderful blessings and confidence in our daily lives, which those without faith cannot replace with the most expensive of material possessions.

To this point, I have been citing the cases on the individual basis; but I feel that collectively we attract negative outcomes when we surround ourselves as a people with negative emotions, news, envy, criticism, entertainment, which seems to be the case in most of the cultural environment we see in the media. When I am asked about all this negativity that surrounds us, I respond that I simply ignore it. I certainly don't focus on it and bring it into my life. It has no place there.

It is my view that if for one week, we eliminated all negative energies within our popular culture and instead focused on good news and positive vibrations, we would see a huge change in the world.

"Every word you utter to another human being has an effect, but you don't know it. If people begin to understand that change comes about as a result of a million tiny acts that seem totally insignificant, well then, they wouldn't hesitate to take those tiny acts." —Howard Zinn

It is also important to see how subtle signs of negativity affect us without our being aware of the negative input. Advertising has become increasingly focused on the implication that without a certain product, you will be unsuccessful, unhappy, unlucky at love, unpopular with peers, etc. Worse are the medical, drug promotions being most frequent it seems. "Feeling tired all the time, consult your physician" rather than "Feeling tired all the time, get more rest." So often wellness comes from simply eliminating negative input and thoughts and insecurities from one's life.

Another helpful way of eliminating the subtle negative input in our lives is to frame our sentences in the affirmative, eliminating as much as possible just that use of the negative structure in our speech. "I don't have time . . ." can become "I have no time." "I can't do" will never allow you to succeed, whereas "I can try" will give you a chance for success.

I suggest that if we wish to change the world for the better, we first need to focus on the positive. How do we do that? Look around and appreciate what God has given us! It's everywhere—we don't have to "manufacture" good news; we simply have to open our eyes and see it. Share love with your loved ones first and foremost. After all, they are the people closest to you; celebrate that. Do things that bring you joy; join other people who share that same energy rather than seeking those that do not.

Eat healthy foods that are good for you. I suggest that a ripe peach off the tree tastes far better and gives you a sense of God's gift to you, rather than spending five dollars for some artificial concoction at some trendy coffee shop. Spend time to go to a concert where people sing uplifting songs and celebrate their positive energies.

Rather than reading of crooks and evil-doers, celebrate those who do heroic actions, thank a veteran next time you see him or her. After all, they are out there working to keep you safe.

Encourage others by word and action to do the same, to manifest positive energies; support those who love their work, their businesses, rather than just going into huge impersonal warehouses to save a couple of dollars. Support your local businesses; after all, they are our neighbors, and we're in this together. It's our neighborhoods, our towns, and our cities where we spend the majority of our time that should be the focus of our attention. When it comes time to exercise your right to vote, vote more for positive candidates rather than simply pulling the same levers. Let's speak out and create a better world, each in our own way. Adopt a pet and nurture it; plant a tree, some flowers; make a difference, a positive difference. We should all aspire to leave the world a better place than when we found it.

To believe God created the earth and everything in it as the Bible tells us requires faith and acceptance of the holy writing passed onto us from centuries ago. There are many who scoff at the idea of faith in the Bible and choose to believe instead everything happened by a cosmic accident or, better yet, a universe that extends outward for billions of light years, which all came from a point of origin so small that . . . it was *immeasurable*, that is, **nothing**. Hmmm. That, they suggest, is "science" or "fact," not *faith*; after all, that is akin to superstition. Man's hubris never ceases to amaze. He knows. He can tell you with a straight face that something came from nothing.

This is the same person who marvels at the precision of his new car's engine or his latest iPhone, or one tetra-megagig hard drive supercomputer, which are in his word *awesome*. Yet the greatest neurobiological minds working to "map" a fruit fly's brain will likely take a decade or more figuring it out. A fruit fly. Yes, that is quite remarkable, well, actually in more ways than one; the first is that we consider awesome and the height of technology and human development, man's creations (no one has suggested that Ford's latest creation was a cosmic accident), and yet dismiss as a cosmic accident the relatively simple brain of a natural creature, so simple that hundreds of the best and brightest scientific minds working together may (it is not yet certain that they will or even can) work out the "map!" Perhaps it could be said that it is quite remarkable that despite our being able to witness every day of our lives evidence of God's creations all about us, we still marvel at our own creations while dismissing God's as accidents. But to suggest that these geniuses could perhaps spend their professional time on less grandiose projects, even smelling the roses, instantly brands one as a heathen, an anti-intellectual, a buffoon who does not respect "learnin'."

It is perhaps even more enlightening to have these same learned individuals finding that the more they seek to disprove God and the Bible, faith, and the spiritual, the more they find themselves confirming otherwise.

No one would suggest that Da Vinci's *Mona Lisa* created itself by some remarkable coincidence of nothing becoming something. Man is very proud of his hand in his creations, yet most are equally ready to dismiss God's hand in the creation of all around us.

They are able to tell someone, for example, who has witnessed a miracle and inform him that he was mistaken, for miracles don't happen, in their worlds, at least. Instead, they should be giving gratitude every day that they are living, breathing miracles of a Creator they don't even want to acknowledge. They're too smart.

It does not take faith to see an airplane being built, because one can go to the Boeing factory and see hundreds of skilled people assembling its millions of components. We can likewise see an anthill a day or so after a hard rain reappearing, rebuilt with amazing precision and effort by a population of tiny insects whose organized efforts at working together exceed even the most efficient of human organizations. We don't need "faith" when we can see something for ourselves.

Yet we were not present at the creation. Whatever explanation we offer or is provided to us requires faith. As we are still a free people and can choose to believe in the Bible or otherwise, and having studied the Bible extensively, I choose to accept the biblical version of creation as God's holy account.

NOTES

NOTES

For I know the thoughts that I think toward you,
saith the LORD, thoughts of peace, and not of evil,
to give you an expected end.

Jeremiah 29 v 11

CHAPTER 7

The Bible and Jesus Teach the Law of Attraction

"Therefore I say unto you, What things soever ye desire, when ye pray, believe that ye receive them, and ye shall have them."
—Mark 11:24

The Law of Attraction is not a magic wand for people to wave and sit back for their imagined Ferrari's and mansions as I hope I have previously made clear. However, neither are poverty and scarcity God's intentions for our earthly circumstance. After all, he created the Garden of Eden for his human likenesses. It is clearly stated in John 16:24: "Hitherto have ye asked nothing in my name: ask, and ye shall receive, that your joy may be full." Prosperity for the faithful is clearly stated in Job 36:11: "If they obey and serve him, they shall spend their days in prosperity, and their years in pleasures." Your redemption includes prosperity. However, in order to receive true prosperity, you must ask and also obey and serve him faithfully.

You may ask why Jesus was born poor if God's intention for us is to be prosperous. After all, that appears a contradiction. But think about this. Jesus could have easily been born in the finest of earthly palaces as befits royalty and could have been wrapped even at birth in the finest silks and woven blankets. After all, he is God, the Son of God; and through the ages, kings have claimed God's sanction for their authority over their earthly domains. Yet in 2 Corinthians 8:9: "For ye know the grace of our Lord Jesus Christ, that, though he was rich, yet for your sakes he became poor, that ye through his poverty might be rich." We all know that there is an enormous separation between the average man on the street and the "royals" as is popular in current press references to today's royal families. There might be popular adulation as we have seen on television with the ceremonies surrounding Queen Elizabeth's sixtieth anniversary on the throne in 2012, but that is different from feeling a kinship, as we do with our neighbor or the average person on the street. By being born into ordinary circumstances, well, even less than ordinary, Jesus did not separate himself from his people—he worked among them, preached among them, and revealed his being the Son of God not through gold and silver and silks and living in a palace but in performing miracles and showing us by example how to follow God's wishes for us to obey and serve God.

Our prosperity pleases God. We read that in Psalms 35:27: "Let them shout for joy, and be glad, that favour my righteous cause: yea, let them say continually, Let the LORD be magnified, which hath pleasure in the prosperity of his servant." It pleases the Lord for those who serve him to prosper as he wishes. After all, he created the earth and all the natural abundance upon it and gave us the ability to act as stewards and gain the riches therein. The key here is that true abundance and prosperity comes from serving him; therein lies *true* righteousness. When one serves the Lord in true goodness, he experiences that spiritual joy that comes from God himself. We can know that joy daily when we sit down at the dinner table and take that moment to pause and express our gratitude for what he has provided. We must remind ourselves that it is this spiritual joy that is the difference between true prosperity and the false prosperity of worldly possessions otherwise. All too often we have seen in others, perhaps even ourselves, that wishing, hoping, striving for something that is in truth simply a worldly possession, a new car or a toy, anything that we think that achieving that goal will bring us happiness, only to gain it and sense a feeling of disappointment. This sometimes is very difficult to understand, but it is very commonplace. I know a man, for example, who takes good pictures but had a camera that was not working as it should after he dropped it. He was having difficulty earning enough to afford a replacement, but it was also necessary to his work. When he finally got a new one, he appreciated its true value to him because it enabled him to achieve what he needs to be able to do. Let's take another individual who wanted a similar camera, they aren't cheap, but when he got it, he just put it on the shelf after a few days and rarely used it. For the latter, receiving what he wanted only increased his possessions without giving him spiritual satisfaction; for the first man, it truly brought him self-satisfaction, and he was grateful for that and prospered. I believe we can see this same point made in Proverbs 10:22: "The blessing of the Lord, it maketh rich, and he addeth no sorrow with it." When we combine spiritual riches and worldly riches, we truly receive what God wants for us with no sorrow or regret or disappointment.

We see that further stated in 3 John 1:2: "Beloved, I wish above all things that thou mayest prosper and be in health, even as thy soul prospereth." This is very important. Reflect a moment on *above all things* and what this states, because this is clear: God's wishes for you *above all* include health and prosperity in this world at the same time that your soul prospers spiritually. In other words, you do not have to deny yourself prosperity or your well-being to be prosperous spiritually by being in God's graces.

Be in God's graces by aligning yourself spiritually with God first, and you can truly attract the blessings of good health and prosperity without the conflict of sorrow. We will examine this in the next chapter, the centering of oneself spiritually, but I wish to offer one caution here that I believe we all face, likely both having seen it in others' lives as well as in our own. Our popular culture today it seems even more than ever places enormous importance on material possessions and so frequently focuses so much on the extravagant display I would call obscene wealth. This is offered to us and our children as entertainment, and I suggest it is insidious in many ways. Obviously, it suggests that these people who have been blessed with these possessions are somehow to be envied and that their displays of arrogance and excess are something to aspire to. Ironically, they also show often the abusive behaviors of some of these same people and their addictions and unhappiness as though these struggles are also "entertaining" to their audiences. However, rarely if ever do I see them asking these people or themselves about the spiritual religious aspects of these people's lives.

I also have to add a cautionary note here before one might suggest that a very wealthy person who "goes to church on Sunday" reveals his spiritual prosperity by his church attendance. Frankly, only that person himself knows that answer, and it is certainly not our role to judge our neighbors in any way. That is God's responsibility and between God and that person. What I wish to caution each of us, though, is perhaps making the mistake of drawing a parallel between material possessions and being blessed, and, in particular, substituting material "gifts" for love and attention to those who need our spiritual attention. In particular, I suggest that sometimes our schedules and demands on our time sometimes make it difficult for us to share the love, spend the time, and give attention to those most important to us. Perhaps a bit more spiritual prosperity, even if it means less material prosperity, is best for our true well-being, not only for ourselves but also for those we love.

As there are those who might suggest that we are in conflict with God's wishes for us by seeking to attract worldly prosperity into our lives and suggest as evidence of this Jesus's being born into poverty, I ask that you think this through given the above evidence otherwise.

I also suggest that you take time to examine the issue of poverty itself as a chosen state for God's children, as others might infer. I truly believe there is a curse of poverty. Jesus shed his blood for our salvation, and this sacrifice included freeing us from any bondage that we were under. Financial prosperity frees us from the bondage of lack and allows us to move from the land of not enough to the land of more than enough. Again, I wish to make it clear that we are not simply defining prosperity as the possession of material wealth but material wealth and abundance in accordance with spiritual centering.

One of God's wishes for us when we are spiritually centered is to bless others with our abundance, to share and assist them in finding their own spiritual paths to God and in escaping the bondage of poverty themselves. You cannot bless others financially if you are broke and poor. You cannot adequately provide for your family and loved ones if you are in financial bondage.

We are all familiar with the parable of the Good Samaritan in Luke 10:25-37. While the priest and the Levite both chose to ignore the victim of the robbers by passing on the other side of the road; the Samaritan, likely also a busy man, stopped and cared for him. Then he took him to the village and paid for his care, instructing the innkeeper to continue and that he would repay him upon his return. We have often read of stories of people either ignoring or caring selflessly for others in need and either feel disappointed or uplifted from reading about these acts. I ask you to think a moment about the parable, and I suggest to you that it just stands to reason that this gentleman could not have helped the other man if he had not had the resources to do so.

Let's once again examine the contention of many who suggest that because Jesus did not have anything, we should not want or desire wealth or nice things either. I believe these people are missing a major point. Jesus had everything and gave up all the riches of heaven to come here and be poor so that we could become rich. Jesus did not want the people who saw him on earth to envy or covet the material trappings he easily could have displayed as the Son of God. He wanted them to again be saved, to gain the kingdom of heaven, and to also renew their faith while on earth. Had he been surrounded by palace walls, it is doubtful the common people of his time would have been able to be as comfortable in his presence as they were in his living a simple life.

We must acknowledge that God is not poor, and we are adopted into his family with full rights to our inheritance. And we do this by believing Jesus died for us and obeying his laws, centering ourselves with him spiritually, maintaining our faith, and attracting and creating prosperity and abundance to ourselves. It is the Law of Attraction that draws this prosperity to us.

You all know of the story of the doubting disciple, Thomas, who would not believe in the resurrection without seeing Jesus in the flesh, John 20:27: *"Then he said to Thomas, 'Put your finger here; see my hands. Reach out your hand and put it into my side. Stop doubting and believe.'"* Because the Law of Attraction is one of God's laws, as I have repeatedly demonstrated previously, and yet as a spiritual law, there will be some "Doubting Thomases" who need to "see" something before accepting the idea of energies and vibrations, and how negative and positive energies indeed can have physical consequences. I wish to show you a brief video that reveals this very clearly. I ask that you, in particular, look at the photographs taken by Dr. Masaru Emoto, who used purified water and focused various thoughts, prayers, emotions, and names, and photographed the water crystals (http://www.youtube.com/watch?v=tAvzsjcBtx8).

One might wish to pay special attention between the three-minute mark of this video for an explanation than at the four-minute mark for the pictures of negative and positive thoughts (http://www.knowledgeoftoday.org/2012/03/thought-definition-life-energy-power.html).

There will be devout Bible-adhering Christians who suggest that the above research should be rejected as being contrary to their beliefs, and they are entitled to their own views, as we all are. However, I again contend that since God created the earth and the universe and everything in it, even if the individuals who are conducting the studies and scientific research do not acknowledge the Bible, if their research is conducted scientifically, they are attesting to God's glory and his creation; and their personal spiritual beliefs do not matter.

I still suggest that rejecting the Law of Attraction for examples such as the above does not disqualify the validity of the Law of Attraction. As the images allegedly revealed, the difference between positive and negative vibrations and energies can affect the physical world. This is a critical factor because if one indeed is attracting negative outcomes through expressing negative thoughts and actions, he is denying himself the same blessings and prosperity God wishes for him. To refuse to acknowledge, this does not diminish the outcome. I suggest that we look into ourselves and ask, Do we feel good or expect good things to happen when we are expressing negative feelings? Are we happy during these times of negative influence? I am not suggesting that there are not bad things that happen, but do we want to *add to them* by attracting more?

Although the following comes from Plato's *Allegory of the Cave* and not the Bible, I believe the tale has relevance in our context.

Basically, there are prisoners in a dark cave. They are chained and can only see shadows on a wall. To them, the shadows are the truth, because that is all they know. They don't realize they are just a shadow of objects that people are holding up against the light of a fire.

A prisoner escapes and makes his way out of the cave. When he sees the sunlight for the first time, it hurts his eyes, and he runs back into the cave. But after a while, his eyes adjust, and he goes back out again. He realizes how beautiful the light is. He begins to realize the cave was not the reality, not the truth, but that the light is what is actually beautiful and real.

The point is that is what living in society is like. If we choose to believe everything people of authority and power tell us, if we accept what we read in the paper or on TV as being the truth, guess what? We're one of those prisoners chained in the cave.

So many injustices in this world will never be first and foremost for government, media, etc. This is 2013; and we still have slavery, child abuse, rampant violence against women, hunger, homelessness, etc. Why? Because too many of us are content to stay chained down in that cave, believing what those with power and money want us to believe.

The above tale was written in 380 BC and still applies today. I believe God does not wish us to live our lives in the caves of negativity, either our own or by accepting that around us.

I believe instead of surrendering to the negativity and allowing ourselves to attract negative outcomes to our own lives, we must renew our faith and truly appreciate and acknowledge God's wishes for us and not attract the troubles around us into our own lives. We can do better. The Bible shows us how the Law of Attraction is God's law and intended for us to live abundant, prosperous lives in keeping with the wishes of God. This is our choice.

NOTES

NOTES

Giving thanks always for all things unto God
and the Father in the name of our Lord Jesus Christ;

Ephesians 5 v 20

CHAPTER 8

Renewing Your Mind

"Nurture your mind with great thoughts, for you will never go any higher than you think."

—*Benjamin Disraeli*

Your life is a garden, your mind is the soil, and your thoughts and words are the seeds. You can grow flowers. Or you can grow weeds. The decision is yours, and it is important to grasp how your very thoughts affect your entire life and well-being, no matter how you otherwise profess your faith in God.

One of the important points that has been stated up to now about the Law of Attraction being God's law is that one needs to be in accordance with God spiritually to gain the intended prosperity. In order to do so, we need to "tune up" ourselves, to renew that sense of our relationship to God and Jesus and the Holy Spirit. This need for renewal of the mind is clearly stated in Romans 12:2: "And be not conformed to this world: but be ye transformed by the renewing of your mind, that ye may prove what is that good, and acceptable, and perfect, will of God." Regardless of our circumstances, we may find ourselves "conformed to this world" and caught up in all the demands on ourselves in our jobs, or families, and the world around us, whether through our surroundings or through the media we invite daily into our lives.

It is impossible to truly be spiritually centered with the will of God when we are distracted, stressed, frustrated, angry, and our minds are otherwise occupied with the world's demands on us. One of the ways I find to renew the mind is to take time to reflect on our faith step by step, reminding ourselves of how God's omnipresence is in all that surrounds us, just as it is within our individual minds, hearts, and souls.

To start at the beginning, how did God create all? The Bible tells us that God created everything by speaking it into existence. What we need to remind ourselves in this biblical truth is that God created everything by speaking it into existence. As God made man in his image, in Genesis 1:27: "So God created man in his own image, in the image of God created he him; male and female created he them," we have the same empowerment in our own lives. We can "speak" our wishes to create our own lives and what we wish to find therein. Yes, we have faith, and this faith and spirituality provides us the strength to know God and trust in him to guide us. However, we also must "speak" our wishes to him. I do not wish to trivialize this point; but when you go into a department store and you want the clerk to hand you something to hold and examine, perhaps to buy, you must speak to him, make the request verbally, "speak" your need. I feel God wishes the same courtesy, that you don't simply utter a silent prayer or statement of faith, but that you "speak" to God that which you wish to attract, what you wish to have him provide.

God is an infinite being. He is perfection itself; therefore, there is no time delay. All he has to do is speak the word, and its fulfillment is instantaneous.

Moving forward, again, Genesis 1:27 states that God created the male and female. Now with that in mind, we know that we are made in God's image and share his characteristics. This should give us a solid base for our self-worth.

However, we must continually renew our awareness that our self-worth is not defined by our possessions. It is not defined by what we drive, how big a house we live in, what kind of toys our children possess. It is also not going to be defined by our achievements, the certificates and the degrees on the wall, the accolades from work, from our business, whatever Our self-worth is also not determined by our physical attractiveness or whether we are popular or famous Our self-worth comes from being made in God's image; and because of the price Jesus paid for us, because we were bought with a price, his blood, is why we can and should feel positive about ourselves.

There is one more point to cover here. God made both man and woman in his image. They are both made equal in God's sight. From the beginning, the Bible places both man and woman at the pinnacle of creation. Neither sex is raised above or placed below the other.

The next point that I would like to bring out is that we know that we are created in God's image, and we know that God is a spiritual being. That means that we are also first and foremost also a spiritual being. We are a spiritual being experiencing a short term of physical presence. This is a very important point to understand in renewing our faith. When we, for example, answer the question, who are you or what do you do with I am a human being or a teacher, whatever, we are focusing on that brief time of our earthly journey rather than the great span of eternity we have existed spiritually and have known God. Many of the problems that we run into in our lives occur because we fail to make that distinction. Most of the time, we tend to look at ourselves as a physical being first. We fail to realize and remember that God created us in his image, and we are therefore an eternal spiritual being. I want to dwell on this for a minute longer. Although we are in human physical form for a brief time, whatever attributes our spirit takes on while here in our physical body will determine where our soul rests in eternity. In other words, if we retain the sinful nature of Adam, we will be spiritual beings eternally dammed. However, if we ask Jesus to forgive us and ask him to be our Savior, he gives us salvation, and we will get to spend eternity in the presence of God.

Knowing you are a person of infinite worth gives you the freedom to love God as well as to know him personally and to be a light to others. When Adam and Eve were created and before their fall from grace, I believe they were perfect and walked with God and knew him personally. Then, after disobeying God, mankind lost this relationship with God for the eons. There was a chasm between man and God that was not in effect closed until the Coming of Christ. During that time, man had to deal with prophets and priests rather than directly with God.

Through Christ's birth and becoming a man, God again gave us the opportunity to know him through Jesus. What Jesus did restored our self-worth, and it was the price he paid that truly revealed the depth of his love for us. This is another very important consideration in our steps to renew our mind, our relationship with Jesus, and giving thanks for his love.

Let us consider our time here on earth and how to live our lives to assure salvation and spending eternity with God. Many times you will see people who are not in the best of health, and it is very obvious after getting to know those persons that it is because of their poor diet and lack of exercise. We see this everywhere we look. It is sad, especially in this nation of such abundance, that people do not take better care of themselves and their health and well-being. They do not give their bodies the nourishment and care their bodies need. Now think of our souls and spirits. Do we take the time to truly nourish our spiritual selves? Because we are a spiritual being, our spirit needs nourishment just as our physical bodies do. It is difficult to be balanced spiritually if all we do is spend an hour at church on Sunday morning as though we are paying our dues to our Father in this manner. Think about this. There are twenty-four hours a day, seven days a week; and if all we give God and our spiritual souls is one to two hours a week, virtually less than 2 percent of that week, it is no wonder that so many of us are spiritually malnourished or worse. How would we fare if we simply ate one or two meals a week? Soon we would be on death's door. Just as we must not starve our physical bodies, we have to feed our spirit daily by renewing our faith and expressing gratitude to God for our presence here and for the love and fellowship we share with family and friends and others we know. I suggest that when we do this, our physical needs will fall into place much easier. How do we feed the spirit? First, we nourish our spiritual beings by praying devoutly to God and reading and reflecting and taking to heart on his words in the Bible. The more we study the Bible and the more we learn about God, the smaller we become as regards our physical selves and the greater we in our spiritual beings sense a communion with God. God says to meditate on his word. The Bible also says in Psalms 46:10 to *"be still, and know that I am God."* Sometimes we just need a peaceful place to relax and reflect on our lives. These are just a few ideas about feeding your spirit and renewing your minds. I believe that you have to talk with God daily if you want to keep your spirit healthy. This does not mean we have to be on our knees in formal prayer many hours out of the day. What I believe he wishes instead is to carry on a conversation just like you would with a friend. In a sense, it would be better to begin practicing this now without waiting for a crisis when you feel desperate, in need, or so all alone that you then find the need to ask God for his help. Don't only express need but gratitude; give him thanks. I remember a crippled man who daily gave God thanks; and when asked why he, in such pain and helplessness compared with the rest of us, gave God thanks so openly and without qualification, he replied, "I give him thanks for being alive and able to know his love." Sure, it may take moments from our day; but I suggest that every minute, every hour spent in God's presence and friendship is the best possible way to spend that time. Rather than surrendering yourself to anger or a sense of helplessness, I believe what God wants from us is to turn to him and rely on his help. But let that not be the only time we turn to him. When we are tempted and need help, he is there. We get into trouble thinking we can handle this, and we don't ask God for help. Then we fall and get discouraged all because we did not ask for help in the first place. And he was waiting just hoping we would call. He is always there, as they say 24/7, but we have to remind ourselves He wants a one-on-one relationship with us. He wants to be our best friend and always be there for us. He wants us to speak our desires and needs, and he will fulfill them, so long as they are right for us.

There is a tool I call a life wheel (see Diagram 1). There are numerous life wheels that show a pie chart in four pieces. One slice represents your spiritual health, one slice is your physical health, another your relational health, and the last your financial health.

DIAGRAM 1

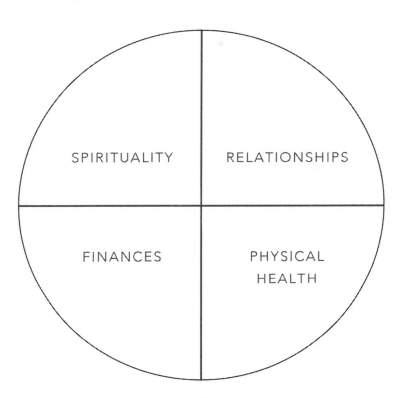

All of the life wheels that I found were like this, just a pie with slices however big or small they were. But I believe if your spiritual walk is just another slice of the pie, then you are already out of balance. As we said, we are spiritual beings; therefore, our spiritual walk has to be centered. Then it gives energy to the rest of our life. If you simply look at your spiritual life as just one slice of the pie, that is very much like having a bubble on one of your car tires. This will cause the whole car to shake and wobble, and it will eventually blowout. Just like tires, our lives have to be balanced.

Our strength and power and vitality all come from God. Therefore, it stands to reason that as it comes from him and then flows through and out from us. This is why I stress that we need to nourish our spiritual being by being in the word and by understanding the need to be around others who hold us accountable and who build us up and provide positive energies in our lives as we do them.

This is what my life wheel looks like, a wheel rather than a pie.

DIAGRAM 2

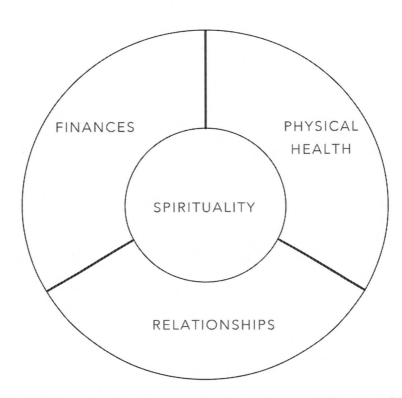

This life wheel shows, just like a wheel, your spiritual life centered in the center hub. This is what I came up with because with the other ones, you would already be out of balance because the spirit was not the center core.

This is what I call centering the core, placing your spiritual life first. This balances your life as you are then allowing God's spirit to flow out and empower and energize everything else we do. Without this, I believe burnout is inevitable. We cannot sustain life ourselves if we do not feed the spirit. Then all we do is exist; that is not what God planned for us. Jesus came so we could have life more abundantly.

DIAGRAM 3

There is a story about a young Indian boy that was about to go through his vision quest. That is a rite of passage for a young boy to become a man. He had a dream one night. In his dream, he saw two wolves come up out of his body and stand over him like they were about to fight. They were snarling at each other. One was a white wolf, the other black, and he could sense that the white one represented good and the black one evil. The next day, he asked the medicine man what his dream meant. He asked if they would fight. After the medicine man said, "Yes they would indeed fight," the boy asked which one would win. The medicine man said whichever one the boy fed the most.

Think about that. Let it really sink in. This is exactly the philosophical thought process that occurs within our minds. Whatever we are putting into our minds is feeding us, the "wolves" within. Which wolf do we wish to feed?

If we constantly feed our minds with negative garbage and with bad thoughts, we will continue to have negative feelings and experiences. In truth, we are unconsciously using the Law of Attraction to attract those negative black wolves to us. It is kind of like planting a garden. I cannot plant corn and expect to harvest green beans, or plant tomatoes and pick bell peppers. We read in Galatians 6:7: "Be not deceived; God is not mocked: for whatsoever a man soweth, that shall he also reap." When I sow my garden, I must expect to reap what I sow. Unfortunately, many times we plant these negative thought seeds, and then we wonder why we are not getting the harvest we had hoped for. This is just common sense, but we still do not realize this simple lesson of life. This is the Law of Attraction bringing us the negative outcomes we have sent forth into God's universe. There is a computer term that says, "Garbage in, garbage out!" Our minds are the same.

Another verse that reveals God's intent for us to renew our minds is found in Psalm 51:10: "Create in me a clean heart, O God; and renew a right spirit within me." By creating that "right spirit" within ourselves, we align ourselves with God's spirit and allow the abundance to come forth into our lives when we speak and ask for that prosperity.

> In Philippians 4:8: "Finally, brethren, whatsoever things are true, whatsoever things are honest, whatsoever things are just, whatsoever things are pure, whatsoever things are lovely, whatsoever things are of good report; if there be any virtue, and if there be any praise, think on these things." Here we are instructed on what thoughts are right and just for us to hold and to think on, in order to renew our minds and align our spirits for God's blessings.

> Ephesians 3:16: "That he would grant you, according to the riches of his glory, to be strengthened with might by his Spirit in the inner man." Here we are again instructed to strengthen our Spirit in "our" inner man. In this way, we will be renewed, transformed, and changed in our inner character to receive our prosperity from God's abundance and love for us.

Although God, because of his being an infinite and perfect being, has the ability to create instantaneously, and he also has given us the power to create, we nonetheless experience a time delay because we live in a fallen world and because we are imperfect beings. In order for us to create, we first have to center ourselves with God's will. When we are centered in his will, then he will give us the ideas, the thoughts, and the desires that are within his plan for us. Once we know what it is we want or are striving for, we need to focus on already having it, how it will feel like when we reach that goal. We must also not fear or express doubt. We must have complete faith and give gratitude both for what we already have and what we will receive. This is a key point in renewing our minds. Without gratitude, the flow of blessings will stop.

I truly felt that God put this book in my heart. And the way it has all come together has been very interesting to watch. I have seen the way he works, how he opened doors that I did not even know about, and how things just have fallen into place. Adam and Eve did not have to renew their minds because their minds were perfect. But after they sinned, all of us have fallen short. We now live in a fallen world. Therefore, we must continually nourish our spirits and center ourselves with God and consider him a friend, developing as best we can a one-on-one relationship with God. Because Jesus Christ came and paid the price for us; by doing so, we can have that intimate one-on-one relationship again. We can walk in the cool of the day with God.

NOTES

NOTES

Keep thy heart with all diligence;
for out of it are the issues of life.

Proverbs 4 v 23

CHAPTER 9

Learning to Be Still
and Know that I Am God

"Be still, and know that I am God: I will be exalted among the heathen,
I will be exalted in the earth."

—Psalms 46:10

God created us with action in mind. We are constantly moving about, often rushing here and there, active from when we wake up until we fall asleep. We like to be in control, we like to make decisions, and we like to call the shots. Many times though, we are trusting in our own or others' judgment instead of God's wisdom. We should always obey him above all others, ourselves included. However, our lives and our surrounding world is filled with distractions, rushing here and there, stressed by things that we think at the time are so important we cannot stop and ask ourselves, "What's going on?" There are times when we should just pause, be quiet and still so that we can hear him speak and give us his thoughts and direction. Because our everyday world is so fast-paced and noisy, it can be very difficult to hear God's voice unless we consciously make the effort to do so. I suggest we tune into God's radio because we need to stay tuned to God, to make sure that our receiver is always on his channel. Think of it. How often do you have the radio on in your car when driving and realize you haven't been paying the least bit of attention to the station? It's just a buzz in the background. But God's wisdom, his thoughts and directions, must be given attention and not just as background. It is very important to have a quiet place and time daily, a place where we can tune out the other frequencies and all the static.

Here are three Bible verses to consider as regards how God assures us of his intent in the law of attracting and bringing prosperity and bounty into our lives when indeed we learn to be still and to listen to him. The following verses are from Psalm 37.

"3Trust in the Lord, and do good; so shalt thou dwell in the land, and verily thou shalt be fed." When we live our faith and follow God's teachings to do good unto others, we will dwell with him, and our needs will be met.

"4Delight thyself also in the Lord: and he shall give thee the desires of thine heart." I like this verse because it tells us to *delight*, to take pleasure in following the ways of the Lord. I think of children and the happiness they express naturally and how so often, as adults, we seem to lose that *delight*, that joy and happiness that we should include in our lives. Here it clearly says that *delight* is the way of the Lord and that he in turn will give you those desires of your own heart, those good things you wish to attract in your own lives, by delighting in serving the Lord. Being true to God, serving him should not simply be an obligation or duty that is difficult and a hardship for you; just the opposite, it should bring you joy and happiness *and* abundance and prosperity.

"5Commit thy way unto the Lord; trust also in him; and he shall bring it to pass." Once more, we see the Law of Attraction clearly spoken herein. Notice his instruction to "commit thy way unto the Lord" for herein lies the key, the commitment to him, not just on Sunday mornings but throughout the day and the week. Do and trust, have faith, and he will bring it into your lives.

I don't want this to sound like the Law of Attraction is an *end-all* for your needs and wishes. We must all remember that we are God's children and that we do not know what he has in store for us. We may have to go through a period of learning, of hardship, that we feel is unjust and unfair, and even believe that God has abandoned us. Nothing could be further from the truth. As I wrote in an earlier chapter, losing a job that produced a comfortable living and having to accept a very low wage in a new field at first appeared very unfair. Yet as it turned out, I learned a new skill, a craft that enabled me to literally in time become my own boss. It was not easy, but questioning

God's intention would in no way have served me. As the saying goes, "God works in mysterious ways."

A teacher spoke to his class of a fable about a man who was traveling in a strange area and needed shelter one night. He was taken in by a poor couple who shared their meager resources with him, fed him well, and even gave him their bed to sleep in. The next morning, he asked God to take the life of their only cow. The next day, he had to again ask a stranger for a place to rest. It was a very wealthy, greedy man who, although he had room in his magnificent home, made him sleep with the animals in the barn and fed him nothing. The next morning, the man volunteered to repair a wall that was crumbling in return and worked all day on fixing it.

The teacher then asked the students whether the man had been fair in how he treated the people who gave him a resting place. To a person, the students responded he was very unfair.

The teacher smiled and said, "In the case of the first night, God had intended to take the life of the husband that next day, but because of their kindness to the stranger, his life was spared and God took the life of their cow instead." The students paused and nodded. The teacher continued, "And the greedy man who treated the stranger so badly, was he fair in offering to repair his wall?" Again, the students all responded that he had no reason to do so. "Aha, the greedy man, if he had repaired the wall, would have discovered a hoard of gold buried below, which would have increased his wealth tenfold. Because the stranger repaired the wall, he never discovered it."

The moral of the above story is that we only know from our point of reference, and what might appear at first to be unjust may be the opposite. We must caution ourselves to never question God's plans for us.

I like to use the metaphor of a caterpillar and a butterfly. If one looked at a caterpillar and did not know the process, he would never be able to see the beautiful butterfly that will one day fly among the flowers. Who can tell? We may be in a caterpillar stage in our lives, or we may be like a butterfly still in its cocoon. There is a growing period that we all have to go through, and this is all in God's plan and his timing for each one of us. So what I think is it is God's way of helping us grow at the right time for each of us, and we must have the faith to accept this. Otherwise, we may derail those plans and not live the life God intended for us.

I mentioned it earlier, but it is certainly appropriate in this chapter where we learn to be still and know God. We sometimes face temptation or decisions that we sense are wrong to make, and the situation may not be easy to resist, whether the occasion is a piece of cheesecake or the temptations of sin. By being still and quiet, almost all of us can hear that little voice within us telling us what to do. Some call that little voice our conscience; I choose to believe that is the actual voice of God, the Holy Spirit telling us what is right to do. It may be friends encouraging us to do something that we don't want to do or know we should not do, but their urging sometimes weakens us to the point that we go against our own self-interest and later regret it. God gives us a moral compass, and that compass is within us. Our parents have given us their thoughts and values, hopefully by instilling the words of God through sharing the Bible and showing us through their own virtues. We also hope that our schools and teachers will do the same, as well as our civic leaders and friends, but more and more, it appears that our popular culture is in conflict with the values of the Bible. Yet I suggest that most of us who have faith in God and the Bible know the difference between right and wrong and that by listening to God within us, by being quiet and knowing him, we will do the right thing, make the right choice, even though it may not be a popular thing to do at the time nor the easiest.

There are some biblical fundamentalists who have criticized *The Secret*, Rhonda Byrne's book, for its suggestion that people who advocate the Law of Attraction have no real ability to respond to the problem of either evil or suffering, their logic being that no one would purposefully bring this into their lives; therefore, the Law of Attraction is flawed (www.challies.com/book-reviews/book-review-the-secret). I feel that I have presented that one need not "purposefully" attract suffering or evil into their lives, certainly; but that it comes in either by entertaining negative thoughts or energies consciously or otherwise, thereby attracting those outcomes. Another example, perhaps more direct, is in dealing with the subject of how one, for example, eats, drinks, and exercises. No reasonable person today can suggest that one who abuses drink or is careless in the quantity and quality of his diet is acting in his own best interest healthwise or worse. One may not focus his energies on "wishing" to have diabetes but, by careless eating and lack of exercise, can be "attracting" that pain and suffering into his life. Sadly, I have known individuals, mothers and fathers, Christians who consider themselves true to their faith, who have either from abuse they have suffered themselves as children, or for undiagnosed or untreated emotional stress or disorders, as well as ignoring the spirit of God's scriptures, have passed on their emotional pains to their children, even without admitting such. We have all heard the saying, "Actions speak louder than words," and this certainly applies as much to matters of faith as to other aspects of our daily lives.

Continuing to evaluate how we may or may not be attracting well-being and prosperity into our lives, I suggest another point of departure with the above critic of *The Secret*. He attacks the writer as espousing selfishness when she suggests avoiding "people who speak about their illnesses or problems lest you begin to think negative thoughts and begin to manifest the negative consequences in your own life." Again, I suggest that the correct interpretation here is that by understanding how negative thoughts and complaints bring about negative consequences, I believe that one can attempt to point this out to those with negative attitudes. However, often those individuals seem to wish for more to complain about. If that is the case, is anything really gained by surrounding oneself with their company? That is for you to decide.

In fact, I sometimes ask people to reflect on the subject of "selfishness" and really examine it. In my experience, "selfishness" can mean that one does things to please oneself. Let us say that the person is "selfish" in his love of God. It pleases him to openly express love for God and the people whom he truly loves. He asks nothing in return. Often "selfless" people are actually "keeping score," and at some point in the future, they expect a "pay-back" for "all they did for the other person." Remember, love is something you give freely from your own mind and heart. In doing so, you are as close to God as you can be. God loves us. He wants us to love him, yes, but not for his glory but for our own well-being. His glory is complete; it is all. Think of the parable of the good shepherd. The shepherd did not regard the safe lambs in the flock any less; he was overjoyed when the lost lamb was found because that lamb was saved from the horror of being killed by the wild animals. Yes, we can hurt God because he does love us, but the hurt comes from his concern for us.

The critic also challenges the author on sacrifice, either financial or personal, saying that "sacrifice makes you . . . (believe) in lack rather than in abundance. She puts you in the place of God, as the one who stands at the center of the universe. The Law of Attraction continues in logical progression until it arrives at the inevitable end result of ascribing divinity to humanity." I feel that by associating the Law of Attraction with Byrne's "secret," the critic errs, because if you center yourself spiritually as I have pointed out previously, you avoid his "inevitable end result"—God's Law of Attraction supersedes the humanistic interpretation, and rejecting God's law does disservice to you whether intentional or otherwise.

He goes on to write, "The law offers no higher power than yourself." I believe otherwise; the Law of Attraction is indisputably one of God's laws and is precisely aligned with his higher power. He gives it to you to benefit you for his glory. Yes, you must understand and accept God's sovereignty, but then don't we already do that by our faith in God?

I suggest that by correctly interpreting the Law of Attraction as God's law, which I believe the critic failed to do, you are accomplishing God's wish for you. By following his logic, you are in fact acting against your own well-being, although you, just as he, might not recognize it until you see the

Law of Attraction clearly in the Bible as I have demonstrated. God clearly wants what is best for you and has provided you his guide in the Bible, so perhaps you should really look for yourself, be still, and know God and avoid others' misinterpretations, which might in fact not be God's wishes but their own flawed logic.

I also think this last suggestion makes a lot of sense, don't you?

The more positive energy that you display to the world around you, the more positive and good results you will receive. Not only is it the "law," but it's a good attitude to display toward God and life and those you love and care for around you!

NOTES

NOTES

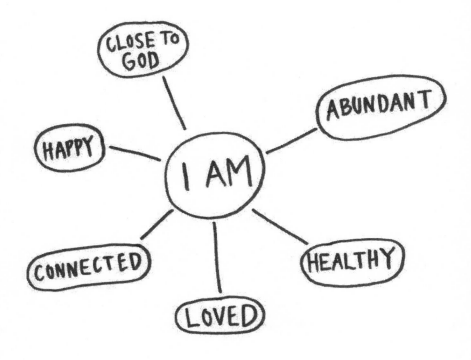

Be still, and know that I am God:
I will be exalted among the heathen,
I will be exalted in the earth.

Psalms 46 v 10

CHAPTER 10

The Power of "I Am"

"What follows the 'I AM' will always come looking for you."

—*Pastor Joel Osteen*

Throughout the Bible, there are so many times when God speaks the words, "I am," and he always speaks in the affirmative, as in "I am the Lord" and "I am thy God" so that the intent is powerful and positive. Jesus also speaks "I am" on many occasions. For example, in Mark 14:62: "And Jesus said, 'I am': and ye shall see the Son of man sitting on the right hand of power, and coming in the clouds of heaven." Here, Jesus uses "I am" to reveal the eternity of God's being and power, in John 8:58: "Jesus said unto them, 'Verily, verily, I say unto you, Before Abraham was, I am.'" In another powerful example of "I am," we read, John 14:6:

> *"Jesus saith unto him, 'I am the way, the truth, and the life: no man cometh unto the Father, but by me.'"* In fact, it would be difficult for me to find in either the Old or New Testament any reference to God or Jesus using "I am" in any way other than to reveal God's power and love in a very positive affirmation. Think about how powerful these simple two words are. "I am."

Again, I remind you that you are created in God's image as we all are, Genesis 1:27: "So God created man in his own image, in the image of God created he him; male and female created he them." To make my point, I have reversed the order of these two verses. In Genesis 1:26, "And God said, 'Let us make man in our image, after our likeness: and let them have dominion over the fish of the sea, and over the fowl of the air, and over the cattle, and over all the earth, and over every creeping thing that creepeth upon the earth.'" Hence, for those of us who place our faith in the word of the Bible as God's own word, there is no doubt here that (A) we are created in his image by his will, and (B) he gave us dominion over our habitat on this earth.

Indeed, man failed to follow God's instructions and fell from grace through the sins of Adam and Eve; but as in the above verse of John 14:6, through our following Jesus, we can again come to be with God so that we can assure our eternal life as well as gain the abundance and prosperity from God in this world. Each of us is able to say, "I am . . . in this life!" "I am . . . loved by God!" "I am . . . blessed by God!" "I am . . . given dominion over the earth to do his will, by God." Think about it; the shortest affirmative sentence in the English language—"I am"—is also the most powerful single statement of all!

Sometimes we simply have to pause and think of those things we so take for granted that the power and importance escape us in our busy lives. Through God's blessings, we have such empowerment over our own lives by literally being alive, of this world, in the shelter of his love and protection.

So how do we so often unconsciously use the power we have been given? "I'm . . . tired . . ." or "I'm not happy . . ." or "I'm not loved . . ." Without giving it a moment's thought, we express negativity, unhappiness, disempowerment, the *exact* opposites of what God indeed intended! I feel that it is important to establish this in every way possible, how any type of negative expression or feeling truly attracts negative outcomes into our lives. None of us wish that, so it is important that we take steps to avoid these occasions by not only recognizing them but also by creating thoughts and sayings to remind us of the power God has given us through the powerful expression, "I am." There are many within the Bible from which to choose, but I am going to select only a few. Should you wish to look at more, the list found here is quite helpful (http://www.divinecaroline.com/self/self-discovery/i-am-what-god-says-i-am).

1 Corinthians 6:19: "What? know ye not that your body is the temple of the Holy Ghost which is in you, which ye have of God, and ye are not your own?" As the verse states, your body is the temple of the Holy Spirit, so you can proudly state, "I am the temple of the Holy Spirit." You are a spiritual being on this earth for a brief time; remind yourself that you carry that spirit within you. This will shield you from times when difficulties mount, and you might otherwise feel a sense of helplessness.

In Matthew 5:14, we read, "Ye are the light of the world. A city that is set on a hill cannot be hid." Our prayer will remind us by simply saying, "I am the light of the world." This is especially important because we can use our light to illuminate the darkness, as in this verse from John 1:5: "And the light shineth in darkness; and the darkness comprehended it not." Not only can we be a light to ourselves but also in reaching out and helping others who may be battling darkness in their own lives.

In John 17:23, "I in them, and thou in me, that they may be made perfect in one; and that the world may know that thou hast sent me, and hast loved them, as thou hast loved me." "I am loved by God."

In one area of health, I fear that many unknowingly contribute to their own lack of good health by their expressions of feeling unhealthy, in pain or diseased rather than stating, "I am healthy as Jesus has taken our infirmities and removed our sicknesses." Here we can see a verse that alludes to this. Matthew 8:17: "That it might be fulfilled which was spoken by Esaias the prophet, saying, himself took our infirmities, and bare our sicknesses." As in all areas of our empowerment and well-being, we are responsible for living a healthy, positive life in keeping with the scriptures, rejoicing in the love of God, and expressing gratitude for our blessings. The Law of Attraction, of bringing health and well-being as well as prosperity and abundance, does require action on our part to accomplish these goals that God wishes for us. The statement "I am" also enables us to assume control over our own domains, stating "I will" and "I can" and following through with these affirmations.

One of the most beautiful expressions of empowerment comes from Colossians 2:10: "And ye are complete in him, which is the head of all principality and power": "I am complete in God the Father, the Son, and the Holy Spirit."

All these empowerment affirmations of "I am" are intended to remind you of your relationship to God and the strength and conviction you gain from your faith in him. You must always remind yourself that your power comes from your personal relationship with God, which you renew daily, and that this in no way requires or suggests that you compare yourself with others. As a true follower of Jesus Christ, you wish to follow his example and reach out to others to assist them in times of need, to share your blessings with them, in a spirit of love and goodness and in honor of God.

Another verse of empowerment is found in Ephesians 1:6: "To the praise of the glory of his grace, wherein he hath made us accepted in the beloved." This verse reminds you, "I am accepted by him." You can feel joyful that you are indeed his friend, his partner; you are blessed.

There is no necessity to choose a favorite affirmation of your relationship with God as the blessings are many and each of us is empowered to develop a personal one. However, I find this one especially gratifying. 1 Corinthians 1:30: "But of him are ye in Christ Jesus, who of God is made unto us wisdom, and righteousness, and sanctification, and redemption." "I am one in Jesus Christ, sharing his wisdom and righteousness and sanctification and redemption."

"I am."

Rejoice and give gratitude to the Lord. Express that gratitude not only in prayer and directly giving thanks to him but also in reminding yourself of that gratitude. "I am happy you're my wife, son, daughter, father, mother, sister, brother . . ." You get the idea; express your gratitude to them. People never get tired of hearing good things expressed to them, good wishes, thoughts, expressions of love. The power of "I am" can be so strong in your daily life.

Even one who may be ill, perhaps terminally ill, can give thanks to the Lord for giving them the time to say goodbye to, in a sense, arrange his life and again express gratitude to those who stood by him. Even the most desperate situation can be alleviated within the glory of God by the statement, "I am at peace with the Lord."

Yes, life can be difficult, and often we do have sudden misfortunes we have a hard time understanding. But expressing a positive statement, such as "I am one with Jesus Christ," can bring one peace he may not otherwise have felt. It is impossible to understand God's plan for us; it is not ours to know but to trust. The power of "I am" is a way to find yourself sheltered by God's umbrella when you need that the most. Always remember, just as Jesus used "I am," so can you.

NOTES

NOTES

Therefore I say unto you, What things soever ye desire, when ye pray, believe that ye receive them, and ye shall have them.

Mark 11 v 24

Chapter 11

Being Ready to Receive

"God has given us two hands, one to receive and the other to give with."

—*Billy Graham*

In order to receive the goodness we wish to attract to ourselves, we have to take our eyes off our problems and focus on what God's word says. We need to reflect and meditate on the word in a positive way. Otherwise, our focus may be on our health issues imagined or real, our financial insecurities, our jobs or careers that we only do in order to earn money and otherwise are unsatisfactory, and similarly unproductive thoughts. In order to receive more, we have to read and study the Bible and learn from God's word for our well-being.

Psalm 78.41 reads, "Yea, they turned back and tempted God and limited the holy one of Israel."

The Israelites limited God by doubting him and his word. God had said this is their land, but they were scared of the beasts and giants living in the land. In the same way of thinking, what are the giants in your eyes today, those things that you fear, which concern you and take your attention away from the positive intent God has for you? Are they your health, the economy, your relationships? What are you paying so much attention to that it comes between you and God? Take off all the limits on God by having nothing between you and him. In this manner, you prepare yourself to become ready to receive him.

We cannot receive what we want until we let go of the things that hold us back. We also must be aligned with God's wishes. Too many times we ask God to help us or give us something, or we say, "God, I am laying this down and giving it up to you." Then when we get through praying, we sabotage ourselves by bending over and picking it right back up. We did not really give it up. Think of yourselves in the supermarket without a basket and you have your hands full. How can you open your hands to take another thing even if it is the gift God wants you to have?

Yet we must *not* consider God as a genie in a bottle waiting around to grant us our wishes. He is the Almighty God diligently working to set the world and his people back to the original state of perfection he ordained for us in the beginning. Either we are on board and part of that plan or we are not. It's just that simple.

Again, you use the Law of Attraction to activate this preparation. For example, if you have a dead-end job or you are just tired of the fact that your efforts are not taking where you want to go, or you feel that you could be doing better, and you feel that it is time for a change in your life, you have to really ensure that you are indeed ready. You may be telling your wife that you are fed up with your career and you feel you can be doing better, but at the same time, you're publicly stating your wish for change. You still hear a voice in your head that may be expressing fear that conflicts with this expressed desire for change. Perhaps it is a voice of doubt or a question about fearing to let go of your "security" because there are so many dangers out there, so many "beasts" that can harm you. You are sending out the message to the universe that you are afraid to succeed and that success will likely elude you.

We hear "success stories" all the time, on Oprah, and "infomercials" that promise untold wealth if you just take such and such a seminar, start this business, etc. Oh, yes, they're "free" to attend, won't cost you a dime, and some of you walk out with a four-thousand-dollar bill on your credit card, suckered into the "success program" second-tier guaranteed six-week Internet course that will show you all the "secrets" that the free seminar did not reveal.

Please do not read the above to suggest that you should not attempt to change, but the important thing is to understand that even though some of these entrepreneurs and successful individuals did indeed achieve their goals, their methods might not work for you despite their "proven success paths." Your goals have to be truly what *you* wish, and you also have to be ready. Then God will show you *your* way, and you will far more likely achieve what *you* are capable of.

So what steps can we take to ready ourselves to receive God's gifts?

———

As I wrote in the previous chapter, you first must take time to be still and "listen" to God. This is so important that I need to repeat it because your mind and attention is scattered among a million different "noises," and some of them are very important, certainly, but others are distractions and prevent us from "hearing" God's voice coming into us. However you best achieve it, practice becoming still and quiet and learning to truly "listen" to yourself and God. God wants to have a conversation with you, both to listen to you and to offer you words and thoughts of wisdom to help you better yourself and achieve your true goals.

There are a couple of phrases that come to mind here, and they are cautionary, not meant to discourage but simply for you to consider, truly consider, the wisdom of your goals, what you wish for. The first is, "Be careful what you wish for . . . ," and also I might add, "be careful why you wish for that goal." We know of the seven deadly sins, although in Galatians 5:19-21, the list exceeds seven:

> "[19]Now the works of the flesh are manifest, which are these; Adultery, fornication, uncleanness,lasciviousness,

> [20]Idolatry, witchcraft, hatred, variance, emulations, wrath, strife, seditions, heresies,

> [21]Envyings, murders, drunkenness, revellings, and such like: of the which I tell you before, as I have also told you in time past, that they which do such things shall not inherit the kingdom of God."

Obviously, we know the consequences clearly stated in the final few words of verse 21. None of us would wish to forfeit inheriting the kingdom of God. Yet at times, we truly have to regard our wishes, for envy and greed can be very subtle, and pride also very deceiving. Sloth and gluttony are very destructive to anyone, and wrath and lust are equally so. However, as an example, we might consider ourselves virtuous and our wishes pure, but remember the two neighboring farmers, one of whom comments as to how God has favored the other by making his farm more bountiful. The prosperous farmer reminds his neighbor that they started with both farms alike. The first farmer's lower work ethic, which he overlooked in his envy of his neighbor, might be not qualify as "sloth," but we are called upon to make our best effort to assist God in providing for us. An individual who wishes God's blessings "to show them" or to "get even" is revealing wrath and is not aligned with God's wishes. Certainly, we can take pride in our accomplishments as well as our goals, but excessive pride or assuming a mantle of virtue or superiority does not fit with God's wishes for us. We do have to question our motives when we are seeking our goals.

In the sense that we must examine our goals, even noble ones, we also have to consider the consequences on others, particularly our loved ones, our family, and our friends. Most often our goals are materialistic, and this is not wrong in and of itself. For if we are penurious, how can we provide for ourselves and give to others? But we must never forget in Matthew 16:26: "For what is a man profited, if he shall gain the whole world, and lose his own soul? Or what shall a man give in exchange for his soul?" None of us is an island or lives in a vacuum. His actions, words, accomplishments, and goals affect not only himself but also others; and he must take into consideration the cost not only to himself but also to the others in his life. A friend told me of a trip he took with his son to show him the baseball parks remaining from when he was his son's age. He was not a wealthy man, and the trip would be a sacrifice, but he saw it through the eyes of his own memories of his father but his son's. One day he told a very wealthy woman of his plans, making the excuse that it might not be financially wise. She replied very wisely and beautifully, "When a man is on his death bed surrounded by his family, he does not regret not making more money, but he often regrets not having spent more time with those he loves."

As you are quiet and listen to God, also listen to what he might say about how your goals might affect those you love. He will reveal to you as much as you are willing to hear. Ask him and listen to his answer.

Now let us assume that his answer reveals that your goal is virtuous in God's spirit as well as for you and those you love. Now trust him to fulfill it and avoid doubt or anxiety about when this might occur. This experience may not take place immediately in most cases because you have to see what steps you have to take personally within emotionally and also what you must externally let go of in order to achieve your goal. But you remain quiet and patient and trust; have faith that you are moving toward your goal.

As you do this, you will begin to understand better the goal you wish and, by listening to God, what he also wishes for you. As the two become one, you will notice how that voice of doubt you have experienced before disappears; you don't hear it anymore. In its place, you feel a calm certitude so that you do not ask yourself "when" but begin to imagine that feeling of success.

Remember, and this is important and has been stated before but bears repeating, you goal is not just a "wish" or something you write on a list for Santa Claus to bring you, sit back, put your feet up on your desk, smile, and feel your work is done.

It may be wise to have a notebook with you in these moments of quiet, so that you consider your goal and then ask yourself to imagine a path between here and there, what you may need along the way. After all, you don't plan a camping trip just by saying, "I want to go to the mountains and lie there and watch the beautiful stars in the universe" without thinking about the trip, the amount it will cost to drive or fly, or what gear you will need to have, and the route, and the clothes you may need in the different climate and altitude, and what you will eat if there's not a McDonald's down the street, and what you will lie on so that you are more comfortable and at peace while viewing God's amazing universe and rejoicing.

When planning any type of trip, one of the most basic items needed is a map. Life is kind of like of like a road trip, including many stops along the way. However, we cannot go into a store and buy a life road map! That is something we have to draw up for ourselves. We need to know what we want, where we want to go, and who we want to take along for the ride.

We create our life road map by setting goals, creating and enacting a plan of action, and then diligently doing our part, working on our plan so that in the end, we can gain our reward, achieving our goal. Using a farmer's field as a setting, we set goals, a bountiful harvest, and we prepare by plowing the ground. In the plan of action, we plant the seeds. Working our plan, doing our part, is weeding and watering the plants that sprout from the seeds. While our reward comes when we reap the harvest, we must not forget to take pleasure in the journey, the steps we take along the way, the plowing, the weeding and watering, watching our plants sprouting, nurturing their growth until they yield the harvest.

Just like the above trip needs details, obviously, too you notice the details in directing yourself toward your goal. By preparing yourself spiritually, you will hear God's voice guiding you toward your goal by showing you which steps you need to take and warn you also which might be distractions. Even what seems "wrong" at the time because it may not have been in your "plan" will be a step along the way, even if it means sacrifice at the time. Remember, God will never ask more of you than you can give. It may be hard, but it's not impossible. I used the example of losing my good-paying job and having to ask my family to sacrifice with me as I worked for much less. Yet what seemed a loss at the time placed me in a position to escape a job that was not what I really wanted and gave me the training that I would need to follow *my* path *prepared* to achieve my goals.

Another observation that I believe is crucial in this process is faith. It is a simple truth but a truth nonetheless. God is perfect and does not make mistakes. Man is imperfect and does. My point is that, just like in the above example of losing my job, my faith was severely tested. Not only was my self-confidence somewhat shaken by being fired, to put it bluntly, but I also had a family to provide for. I was no longer a twenty-year-old young man who could just put his things in his duffle bag, hop in his pickup, and get another job down the road. I had responsibilities to others as well as myself. One thing I did know was that God took care of those who took care of themselves, and I needed to get another job. The times weren't the best either as jobs were scarce in my area, particularly one that paid anywhere near what I had earned previously. I now have the perspective of looking back and seeing God's wisdom far more clearly than I had during the days where I was out knocking on doors and finally accepted a job that only paid a third of what I had been getting. Yes, God tested me, and I'll admit I was scared. But by taking the job that I otherwise would not have considered, I was able to be trained to develop the skills necessary to become a craftsman, working with the wonderful woods available around here. God had tested my faith and had provided me a whole new life, one that made me far happier because it was not just a job anymore but a life's calling.

So sometimes being ready does not just mean opening the door and seeing that man from "Publisher's House" telling you you had just won a million dollars a year for life or some other beautiful fantasy. Being prepared, ready to receive God's bounty, means above all centering your faith so securely that you have no fear, no doubt that whatever happens to you is God's will for you, and however impossible it seems at the moment, trusting in your faith and keeping your chin up, making the best of the situation, knowing that God is there for you. Remember, no matter how bleak or awful or tragic the moment seems, he will never test you beyond your ability to withstand it, so long as you maintain your faith and trust in him. I do not want you to think that I am suggesting that terrible things do not happen to us. They do. Romans 8:28: "And we know that all things work together for good to them that love God, to them who are the called according to his purpose."

But if we do not truly understand the role of our faith and spiritual being, and ignore the lessons in the Bible that provide us the path, if we despair or feel we can set our faith aside for Sunday morning just like the "church-going" clothes we put on, we are not preparing ourselves spiritually to follow God's wishes for us. We can exercise and eat a healthy diet, do the best in our jobs, say we love our wives and children, and have money in the bank; but if we are following man's "prescriptions" for a better life rather than following the Bible's, we are not on the right path for attaining God's abundance. Trust in the Lord and accept that the Law of Attraction is one of God's laws. Center your life spiritually first, maintain your faith in God so strongly that it will be a shield against any adversity, and trust that God will lead you along the proper path to your own salvation and that your love for your own will show them the light as well. Be ready to receive.

NOTES

NOTES

The liberal soul shall be made fat:
and he that watereth shall be watered also himself.

Proverbs 11 v 25

CHAPTER 12

Using Your Blessings to Bless Others

"The quality of your life is in direct proportion to the quality of your relationships."

—Anthony Robbins

One of my favorite sayings comes from Joel Osteen: "Be ready to be a blessing. One word of encouragement can change the direction of a person's life." Up to now, the lesson I have been encouraging you to accept is to understand and appreciate how the Law of Attraction is indeed God's law, and the Bible reveals this to those who wish to find it and benefit through God's blessings.

However, we know through the lesson of Christ that God intends for us to use our blessings to bless others. After all, he sent his Son to live and dwell among us *not* as a king or a rich man but as an ordinary carpenter and preacher, so that we could see his true holiness and humanity and bless us with his presence and teachings and miracles. Jesus shared his blessings with us because God wanted to give us a second opportunity to see for ourselves his glory and reveal through his Son how we could find our own salvation beginning here on earth and extending into heaven as one of his chosen.

We also have the lesson of the Good Samaritan, which I covered in the previous chapter but will again mention, for here was a man who could have easily passed by the injured man and continued on his way as the others had done. Think about it. He was likely busy, had appointments to keep, had obligations, expenses of his own for himself and his family. He had many reasons to go right on by, yet he did not. He rendered aid; he interrupted his day and saved the man's life. Yes, the Samaritan was a man of means blessed in this way. Yet he took money—yes, a blessing of his—and offered the owner of the hostel money to care for the injured man; and if it cost more, he would reimburse him on the return trip. The Good Samaritan in truth shared his blessings with a stranger, a man in need, and did so in such a way that his sharing has served as an example for us Christians to this day!

God not only sent his Son to live and dwell with us but to suffer the torture of crucifixion, certainly one of the most painful and humiliating forms of execution, to demonstrate to us how each and every one could experience salvation. For Jesus died as a common thief and three days later ascended gloriously into heaven to sit at the right hand of his Father. God, through his Son's life on earth, shared his blessings with us in the most profound example of blessing others one can imagine. We have heard of this in combat, perhaps known a person whose life has been saved by another's sacrificing his life for what the soldier considered a greater blessing, saving the lives of his fellow soldiers. We have heard of pilots who could have "bailed out" but stayed at the controls of a doomed aircraft so that they could guide it away from homes and populated areas, at the cost of their own lives. Life is full of heroism when we open our eyes. But it is up to us to understand that God intends this, that he wishes us to use our blessings to bless others.

We also have to consider our blessings and not overlook what they are, particularly if they are not material blessings we can put a price to. It has happened to us all, I am afraid, that we are so busy with something, work, a meeting, something that is requiring our attention, that we ignore those closest to us or worse, try to give them a material "gift" while that blessing we should be sharing is our love, our attention, and our consideration for them. Obviously, there are times that are so demanding that we must focus on a priority that we are obligated to fulfill. A doctor, for example, who is called away from his daughter's ballet recital for an emergency operation, certainly has an excuse that cannot be ignored. In a sense, the doctor is "sharing" the blessing of his surgical skills with a person in critical need of those "blessings" in order to survive. However, when he is back home, he can share time with the daughter whose feelings were hurt by the disappointment of her father's absence. It might take a bit of time away from his golf game or a restful moment he needs, but the blessing of family love should be considered one of God's greatest blessings we have all received. A friend described to me how at the moment of his son's birth, which he attended, he became aware of a sense of love that he had never experienced in his life before, as though he had walked into a new room he had never been to. He then told me how he also was grateful because this gift from God was one that the richest and poorest among us could receive and experience, because it was not a "gift" that could be bought yet transcended the finest of material possessions. We sometimes must remind ourselves that God's love, which he has shared with us, is our greatest blessing and that we must also share that blessing unconditionally. The most beautiful discovery we make when we share this is that this love grows exponentially through our sharing our blessing.

There is an example I will borrow from Rick Warren's blog, which I found at this site, http://www.purposedriven.com/blogs/dailyhope. I am going to take a few liberties to dwell perhaps more in an affirmative manner, but first his example.

> You can have all the right equipment to defeat habitual sin in your life, but it won't matter without the Holy Spirit. Imagine you were walking on the beach and saw a dead seagull that had died less than a minute earlier. If you pick it up, it won't be much different than its live counterparts. It'll still be warm. It'll have the same muscles, bones, feathers, and wings. But if you toss it up in the sky, it'll drop right back down to the ground.
>
> Why? The seagull has no life left. The life isn't in the feathers, wings, or bones. It's in the life God puts in it. Without a spirit, the bird won't fly, even if it has all the right equipment.

This reveals a profound lesson and yet a very simple positive one, and that is in learning that God's Holy Spirit is his greatest blessing to us and simply centering it to guide our actions. As Rick Warren's example shows, the difference between the dead seagull on the beach and another flying above is this Holy Spirit, this life force and energy, this love of God and God's Holy Spirit that makes our life blessed.

God blesses us through this Holy Spirit. We must always remember this for without it, our lives cannot achieve the happiness, the abundance, the spiritual joy that God's love does. How many times do we see extremely rich, powerful people, successful entertainers are a sad example, whose lives are in disarray despite their material "blessings"—it is truly tragic that they have so centered their lives without regard for who blessed them in the first place. We are cautioned to never compare ourselves with others because each of us is blessed differently. So if we happen to have been blessed with a talent to play sports at a high level or sing or dance, or are very intelligent and clever, if we assume we are somehow "better" than others and behave in that manner, are we truly giving God his due if *we* are crediting ourselves for our "superiority"? Obviously, the culture we have created may "reward" us with greater material abundance, but truly, can you be happier having ten cars when one is all you can drive at one time? Will buying a larger house to show off your success really make you happier? I do not want you to conclude that I am in any way criticizing worldly success or abundance, but I am saying that the answer to these questions can only be answered by each of us, and I suggest that it is whether the Holy Spirit truly resides within the person materially blessed. I can use the example of a former basketball all-star who resides nearby who was blessed with great physical and intellectual gifts as well as with great worldly abundance. He and his family live in a wonderful house, and I am sure he has several cars. But he also has used his worldly blessings and his spiritual blessings to found and support an academy to teach others. He has also given both his financial support and his recognition to other worthwhile community efforts. There are many examples like this, where those who are blessed have used those blessings to bless others.

But to return to the seagull analogy of Rick Warren, it is the life force, the Holy Spirit, that motivates us, sustains our lives and well-being, and that truly brings us happiness and abundance. Without it, prayer, material success, another car, or a bigger house won't enable us to "fly" any more than the dead seagull can.

I ask you to remember one more thing from this lesson; and that is it is what is within us, the Holy Spirit, that determines our being truly blessed. Time and time again, as I have already shown in previous chapters, those who came to Jesus in need, often mistreated, lame, impoverished, the least "blessed" in their worlds, were healed and made whole through Jesus because he saw within them their need of him. They were not turned away. We may believe that we can do it ourselves without him, but we only deceive ourselves. We may be good "actors" and attend church and appear prosperous and pillars of the community, but to be truly blessed, we need to center our spirit with God's. The beauty of this, just as in the parable of the Good Shepherd, is that if we are lost and missing the Holy Spirit, we can always seek and find his blessing, and he will rejoice along with us at our returning to his flock. It is never too late, but we must seek him and ask for his blessings, and once we have been blessed, use those blessings to share with those around us.

The following example I found at this website and feel it is also very relevant (http://giveattentiontoreading.wordpress.com/2008/10/02/2-corinthians-8-9-blessed-to-be-a-blessing/).

The writer states it so well I will quote it for you and comment afterward.

2 Corinthians 8-9: Blessed to be a Blessing

"And God is able to make all grace abound to you, so that having all sufficiency in all things at all times you may abound in every good work. As it is written, 'He has distributed freely, he has given to the poor; his righteousness endures forever.' He who supplies seed to the sower and bread for food will supply and multiply your seed for sowing and increase the harvest of your righteousness. You will be enriched in every way to be generous in every way, which through us will produce thanksgiving to God."

2 Corinthians 9:8-12 (ESV):

"God has not blessed me so I can hoard what I have been given. Certainly, as Ecclesiastes taught, I am allowed to enjoy my blessings. But, I must remember that the main reason for which God has blessed me is so I may be a blessing to others."

This is not the health and wealth gospel that performs good deeds selfishly only to receive more. No. This is the true gospel that points out God entrusts more to those with whom he can actually trust more. So often, we want and want and do not have because we only want for ourselves. We will be amazed how much God will bless us if we simply become channels of blessings to others.

Of course, when I am not selfishly concerned about what I have and only about how I can help others, if God is not blessing me with something, I'm still content. The question is not how much I have, but how am I helping others.

I know this is tough to remember when every newspaper and television show is warning us that the sky is about to fall in financially. But this is God's will for us no matter what our nation's or the world's economy.

As the writer stated it so well, I feel all I have to add is "Amen!" and focus on the last paragraph because I feel that this is the root of many problems and we have to understand this clearly.

Our popular culture affects us daily in I believe a very negative way that many of us do not truly recognize. I will use the analogy of a person who has a drinking problem but has yet to admit it. Until that person accepts that he or she must avoid drinking, his life will not change for the better.

In the same way, I feel we have to see how negatively focused so much of the media and culture really is and how we need to recognize this to strengthen our lives and perhaps even begin to make a positive change if enough of us work toward that goal.

Again, I use the term "recognize" as becoming aware, because sometimes we may not really "see" the problem because it is too close to us. All we have to do is turn on the TV to watch how many commercials are intended to make us unhappy about our own lives. Of course, they do not say this, but they show us ways to "improve" with little concern for our spiritual well-being. They want to sell us drugs, which often have more side effects that are worse than what they might be curing. Even so-called Christian-based media will seek to make us insecure and unhappy by suggesting calamity and disaster that will doom us, unless we follow their "financial steps"—which certainly will enrich them! We must also take caution when confronted with "patriots" clamoring for conflict—our nation's resources, its well-being, its sons and daughters, should not be sacrificed to simply enrich the greedy, but to truly safeguard ourselves and the blessed nation our forefathers intended for us. We are the empowered, and it is in our faith that we show that strength. We must be prudent and wise in how we act. We must not be "herded" as frightened sheep but banded as brothers and sisters in righteous causes when necessary. For there are very deceitful individuals within our midst, and they can be very persuasive in asking us to sacrifice for ignoble causes in which they seek to enrich themselves.

Walter Kelly once wrote in his comic strip, *Pogo*, "We have met the enemy and he is us," which is so true, us as a people, not as individuals.

I ask you this one question, "Do you think God wanted his sons and daughters to suffer and be miserable, to be impoverished, to be continually at wars and destroy the beautiful earth he created?"

I believe man has only himself to blame for this; and he continues to do so because many can and do profit from greed, pestilence, conflict, and sin. I believe this contrary to God's vision for us.

I use the term "moral compass" to suggest that both as individuals and as people, we must guide ourselves by our moral compass, which orients our own morality with God's. Frankly, we know that many people do not, and I consider this our nation's problem at this point. Until our moral compass points to God, we will continue to be misguided and lost, with many voices claiming to be the "true north" with no regards for the morality as a nation, we follow.

I ask you to not dwell on man's faults and errors but to dwell on God's goodness and follow his path, his Holy Spirit to guide you to the abundance and blessings he wishes for you. There are many words already written on how I believe the Law of Attraction provides us the means of achieving this after we center ourselves with his Spirit and turn our lives over to him.

I also suggest to you that one of the ways you can share God's blessings is by speaking out in affirmation of God and against the negativity that surrounds us. Remember, God also helps those who help themselves, and it is up to each of us to become active in our positive approach to our own lives through God's Spirit and will.

I believe too that in renewing our faith and centering ourselves, we will become stronger through his Spirit so that we will open ourselves to appreciating the lessons God is teaching us through scientific discoveries. After all, God created the universe and all within it. To fear science will "destroy" God is a foolish fear of superstitious weak man, for God created all, including man's curiosity. Obviously, man can err as Adam and Eve did, and many have done since. But the greatest error is to believe man can survive without God. By centering yourself and truly manifesting faith in God, you need not fear inquiry and learning what science has to report. Your faith and centering will remove that fear and replace it with the ability to judge for yourself. After all, you are in God's shelter. There is much beauty to discover, and even the pictures of the universe taken by the Hubble telescope are testimony to God's amazing grace.

True science is the discovery of God's universe, perhaps particle by particle, energy, and pulse. It is man who seeks to sometimes "limit" God, and that is like a man seeking to stop the rain or still the wind. Only God can command the seas and the zephyrs.

Many scientific discoveries are confirming how God's energies and vibrations are indeed the fabric of the entire world around us. Science is just confirming God's omnipotence that is beyond even the most brilliant, holiest man's comprehension.

We do have God's word in the Bible. It is all there. Through our faith and combining our energies and good vibrations, we can begin to shift the direction we are drifting and reorient ourselves as God intended.

Remember, if you will, this one final message from http://www. bible-knowledge: "When God puts love and compassion in your heart toward someone, He's offering you an opportunity to make a difference in that person's life. You must learn to follow that love. Don't ignore it. Act on it. Somebody needs what you have."

We are truly blessed, and the Law of Attraction will bring God's blessings for us and for us to share with others. We must never forget our identity as children of the King of Kings. Regardless of your circumstances, poor or wealthy, it is who you are spiritually that enables you to be received into the kingdom of heaven. God will see through to your true spirit, just as Jesus saw the son of the nobleman disguised and asked him to remove his cloak. Be true to yourself in God's Holy Spirit.

To God be the glory.

The end.

NOTES

NOTES

The 4B was my great grand father's cattle brand. It was first registered in Blanco county Texas in 1880. His name was Hiram Brown his nickname was Hye which is Gaelic for blessed. As I was working on the content and info to build this website I wanted a trademark logo.

I had been trying to come up with something and was mentally blocked. I looked up from my desk and saw the old branding iron hanging on my office wall. It is a perfect logo because on my blogs I talk about the four main balance points of life. Your Spiritual balance, your Physical balance, your Relational balance, and your Financial balance. So there you have it the 4Bs.

I have been blessed to have been raised and live on the family ranch our land was bought by Hye in 1907 and my Father was born here on the ranch in Nov of 1924 and is still running cattle with the same blood line from when Hye Brown started here in 1880. Hye was my Dads mothers Father.

Made in the USA
Middletown, DE
24 September 2015